DISTANT … DAYS IN BURMA and CHINA

with letters, a diary and photographs

Elizabeth Tebby Germaine

Published by Anona Publications in 2013

ISBN 978 0 9926694 0 9

Printed by Book Printing UK
Remus House, Coltsfoot Drive,
Peterborough PE2 9BF

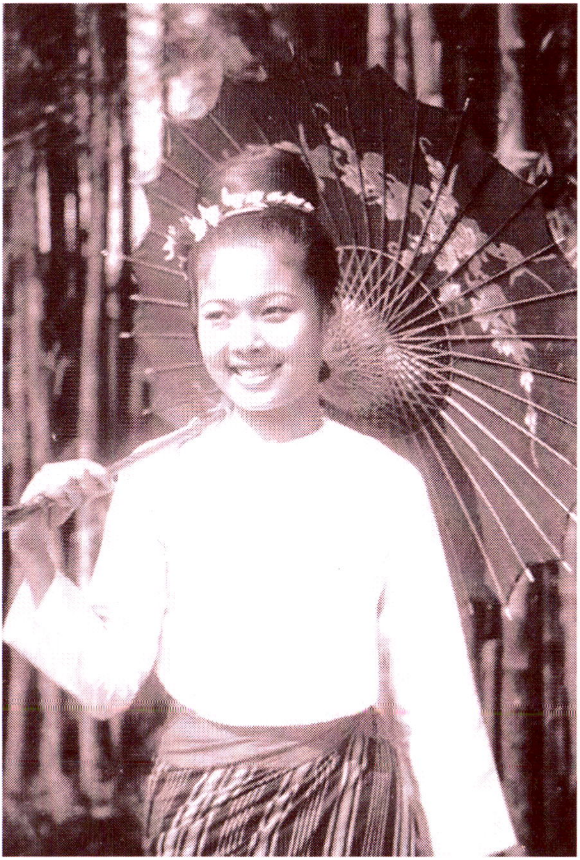

ACKNOWLEDGEMENTS

I would like to thank:

my husband John for his support and practical assistance in putting this book together and our shared interest in the Far East and World War 2, my cousins Tom and John Leach and Anne Wynne for material and photographs they let me have about their parents' time in China from 1926, with memories about the family's journey home from China in 1943,
J R Manning and Dr.E Eason for their articles obtained with permission from the Burma Star website,
John M. Ellis for writing a vivid account in 2012 of his experiences fighting in Burma in 1943-45,
my nephew Dr Michael Lewis for his stunning photo of the Shwedagon Pagoda at night used on the front cover of this book, and other photos of Burma taken in 2012,
my brother Dr David Lewis and Rosemary for photos of old paintings and drawings of Burma and photos taken in 2012,

and Oliver Wendell Holmes (senior) 1809 – 1894, American physician, poet, lecturer and author whose words I borrowed at the end.

An old drawing of the Royal Palace and moat in Mandalay

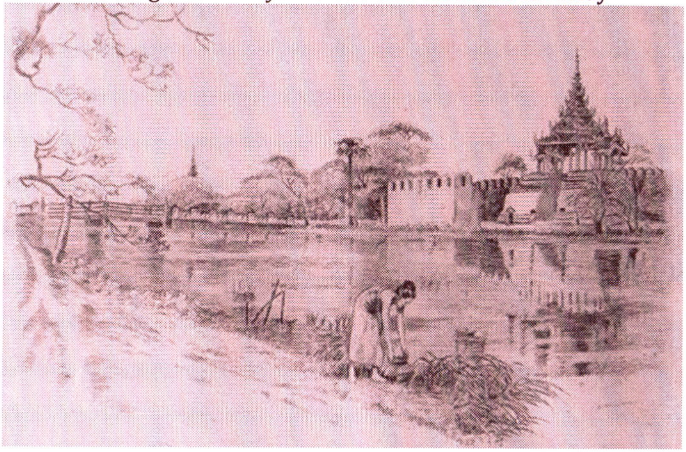

An old painting of Inle Lake

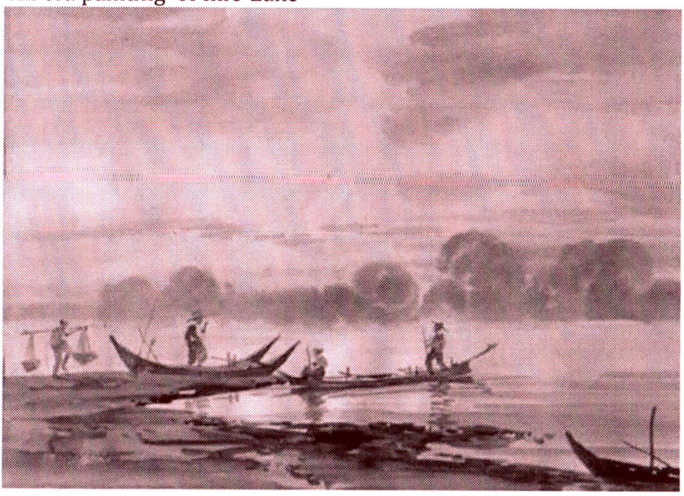

Burmese script

ဟိတ်မင်းတပါးကိုရရှိသဖြင့်။ကျေးဇူးရှင်ပလ္လင်တော်သို့ ရဲရင့်
စွာချဉ်းကပ်ကြကုန်အံ့။
(ဝန္ဒက) ငါတို့ ခံရသည့် သန့်ရှင်းသော ဝိညာဉ်တော်
အားဖြင့်၊ ဘုရားသခင့်မေတ္တာတော်ကို ငါတို့စိတ်နှလုံးထဲ၌
သွန်းလောင်းတော်မူပြီ။
(သန့်ရှင်း၊သူ) ဖြောင့်မတ်သူအထိမ်းအမှတ် ကာလအ
စဉ်တည်လိမ့်မည်။သူတော်ကောင်း၏အမည်ကားလည်း၊ မင်္ဂ
လာတည်း။

၁။ နှိုးဆော်ချက်။

ချစ်ဆွေတို့။ဘုရားသခင့်လက်တော်မှခံယူရသောဆုကျေး
ဇူးတော်များအတွက် ချီးမွမ်းရန်။ ဂုဏ်တော်ကို ထောမနာပြု
ရန်။တရားတော်ကိုကြားနာရန်။ကိုယ်စိတ်နှစ်ပါးအတွက် လိုအပ်
သမျှတောင်းလျှောက်ရန် အကြောင်းများကြောင့်။ စည်းဝေး
ကြသော အခါ။ ပြစ်မှားမိသော အပြစ်များကို။ မျက်မှောက်
တော်တွင်မဖုံးမကွယ်ဝံ့တဲ့။ နောင်တရသောသဘောဖြင့် နှိမ့်ချ
စွာတော်ပြ တောင်းပန် အပ်ကြသည်နှင့် အညီ။ ပရိသတ်တို့
သည် ရှေ့ပလ္လင် တော်သို့ ချဉ်းကပ်၍။ ဖြူစင်သောစိတ်၊ နှိမ့်ချ

Friends *'in a Kachin roadside café'* (northern Burma

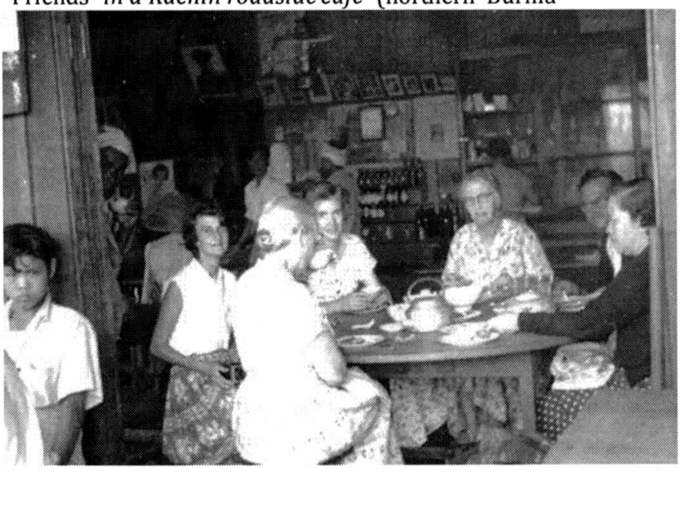

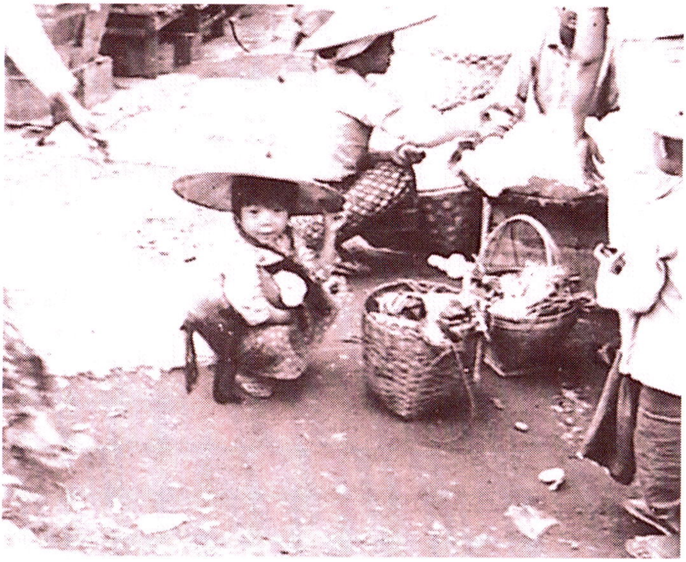

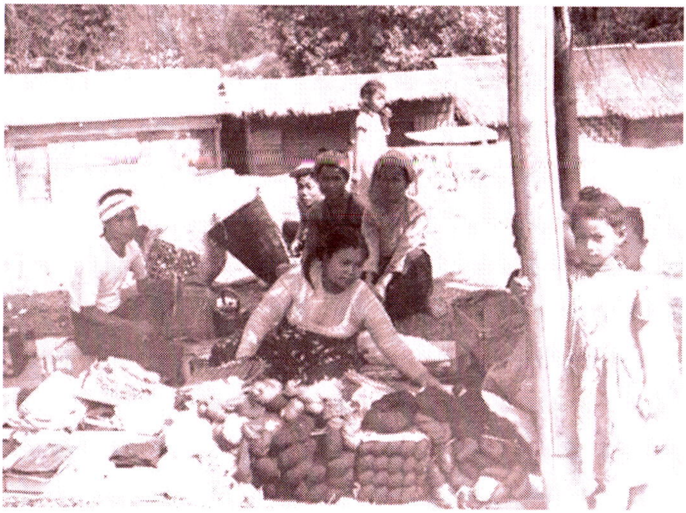

INTRODUCTION

I had a shock. It was 2007 and suddenly there were television images from Burma after years of silence. Thousands of people led by many monks were demonstrating against the regime though of course much that was going on behind the scenes was not visible. In a strange way which is hard to explain I felt close to that mysterious far off land and yet its people were frighteningly isolated from the world even though we now could actually see events that were happening.

It affected me particularly because during our childhood somehow *Burma was always in the background*. Our parents had met there when they were working as missionaries and my brother was born in 1948. I was born soon after they got back to England in 1951 after a calm sea voyage which must have contrasted with what they had left behind. There were pieces of elegant laquerware and pretty sunshades in the house and paintings and drawings of Burma on the walls. As yet undiscovered by me was our mother's detailed diary about her escape from the Japanese invasion in 1942 and a Greek bible on a bookshelf that had its own story to tell.

When they wanted a private conversation our parents would talk to each other in the quiet melodious Burmese language with much laughter and mysterious looks. They kept in touch with people they had known and there were visitors to our house such as the Revd. Peter Ba Maw, Saw Po Kin and Bishop George West and his wife. Reading the diary years later I realized I had often heard the names of many people mentioned in it. I somehow absorbed their love of the country and their sadness when it was difficult to return.

Seeing the report of this demonstration in 2007 and knowing of the terrible suffering going on made me want to do something. It dawned on me that I had some original material lying around that I could try and sort out. It was from another era, longer ago than the number of years, the last days of the British Empire and the terrible times during World War 2, followed by the uncertain years in Independent Burma before the beginnings of the military government.

Old documents left by my family give glimpses into a very eventful and dangerous period in history. It is true that I have included some old and new images which in many cases I find very beautiful, so to a certain extent this gives a romantic view which contrasts with so many shocking events that have happened.

Burma is a country that rarely hits the headlines. The important thing is - what would the people in this story think if they were here now and could see these television images? Like everyone they would feel utter horror.

I had come to a point in my own life where there was time to look at everything and reflect, time to read about what had been happening when these letters and the diary had been written, and time to scan images onto a computer screen. It was a fascinating process to start seeing the detail. Sometimes there was clear writing on the back of the photographs, sometimes it was unclear and I had to try and find things out. Often there was nothing at all. I had been keeping boxes of these old slides and photographs most of which were taken by my father's sister, Aunt Dorothy who had also worked in Burma between 1937 and 1966.

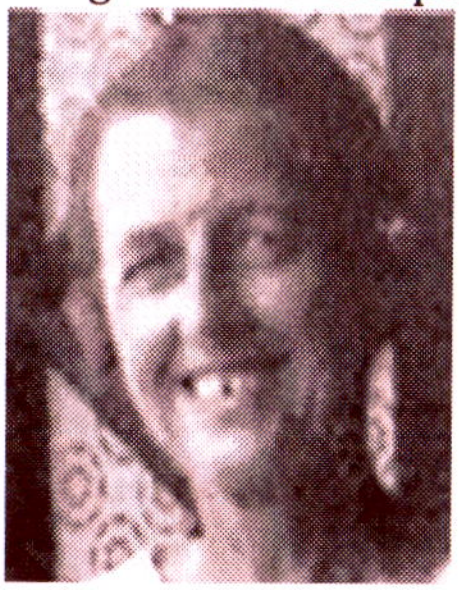

And there was another story parallel with my mother's, of her sister Marian who had travelled to China in the 1920's. As a child of nine I had met Aunt Marian and Uncle Joe a few times but then we moved away and later on I never thought to visit and find out about their experiences.

I had read our mother's diary when she was alive but never asked enough questions and now it was too late. She was always matter of fact about it just as they were all matter of fact about travelling thousands of miles to spread their faith in the Far East. I feel a huge respect and awe that they were driven by such strong faith to travel so far into the unknown, despite my own nagging thoughts that within long standing ethnic struggles in Burma there are also religious conflicts in what has for hundreds of years been a strongly Buddhist country. As soon as I started to study them the old photographs of Burma gave a strong impression that the plain functional architecture of the British built churches and schools contrasted oddly with the stunning beauty of the ancient Buddhist pagodas and temples.

By pure chance I discovered an old battered copy of a fascinating book *'Mowrer in China'* by Edgar Mowrer, an American who travelled in China in the 1930's. He vividly described the suffering of the Chinese people, the changing attitudes of foreign powers who feared that their spheres of influence were under threat, and the growing resistance and strong patriotism that developed during the Japanese occupation. After seeing the film *'The Last Emperor'* I acquired the book *'Twilight in the Forbidden City'* by Reginald F Johnston, the tutor of the boy emperor, a truly amazing and detailed record of the final years of the Qing Dynasty.

I found much old film footage on YouTube about China in the 20th century. I read parts of Michael Sheldon's biography of George Orwell and postponed for the moment a reading of *'Burmese Days'.* I already had a treasured copy of Aung San Suu Kyi's *'Letters from Burma'* and had read with disbelief Emma Larkin's *'Everything is Broken'*. There was tragicomedy in Tony Wheeler's account of his visit to Myanmar in his book *'Bad Lands'* and Ian Buruma's *'God's Dust – A Modern Asian Journey'* was fascinating and complex.

To begin with Josephine and Dorothy and her brother Christopher were living and working within the protection of the British administration. They spoke fluent Burmese which must have been hard to learn, though it was only one language amongst many. In the diary we can see evidence of colonial life where PWD (Public Works Department) bungalows seem to have been built in many widely scattered locations and sometimes DSP's (District Superintendents of Police) are mentioned.

When they arrived in India there were safe places to go and food to eat despite reports of the times of famine and civil unrest. Letters from home reached them there even in wartime. Later our mother's letters from Burma in 1948/9 reveal a happy and productive time but it was now independent and the dangers of civil war suddenly came very close, forcing them to flee with almost no belongings except food for the baby.

As all of this started to come together there were many themes running beneath the surface. My grandfather was a remote and fascinating figure who died 24 years before I was born, and I discovered that he had been awarded an OBE and had been buried in 1927 with full military honours. One day a friend suddenly recalled that she had an uncle who had fought in Burma in 1943-45 and he kindly agreed to write an account of this experience which brought my brief summary of the Burma Campaign to life and emphasized the great contribution made by African soldiers.

When I saw the first surviving letter Marian wrote from China I was stunned by how much was in it, and the remarks made by her language tutor, Mr Pei opened a door into history – there was the sheer barbarism of how foreign powers behaved and the complexities of attitudes to the West and Christianity. The events in history were fascinating and terrible. Each chapter contained enough material for a book in itself. There were constant dilemmas about what to include and what to leave out, where to start and where to end. Nothing is the beginning, there was always more that had happened before.

I selected what I thought to be significant and interesting while being uncomfortably aware that I was skating over the surface of events. The history is there to link the original documents together. Much has been understated through the fragmented records which have survived. The diary is the longest and most detailed old document in the book and is presented exactly as it came to me with no changes, just with comments added. Danger, death and destruction are mentioned but not dwelt upon. There is only one place where Josephine seems to have made a mistake when she writes that the magnificent Gokteik viaduct was destroyed soon after she saw it – this is not the case. There is a film on YouTube of the train travelling on this amazing structure.

With the photos there were some significant finds such as the plan of the old Mission Compound in Mandalay, painted by a Burmese artist. This is one of the places described in the diary when the fires were burning after Japanese bombing. There was a photo on the back of which was written *'Christians celebrating Holy Communion in an air raid.'* I began to see connections between the photos and the story - of course few of the photos are an actual record of moments in the diary but there are some that seemed to connect closely with it. The people are what interested me the most.

A photo of tired children sitting by a river reminded me of the time when adults and children waited endlessly for boats overcrowded with refugees. Some images are of particular historic interest such as *'two racing canoes on Mandalay Moat Jan 16 1937 (Viceroy's visit)'.* There is a photo that matches exactly with - *'...country boats, hollowed-out tree trunks which could take five people.'* I found a photo of Kappali Church and a short article by Bishop West: – *'... The war over, General Aung San, while fighting still for Burma's Independence came to Kappali to see what it was all about....'*

I was given permission by the Burma Star website to quote extracts from two other accounts about similar escapes from Burma through the dense jungle written by a soldier and a doctor. There were striking parallels with my mother's account. And amongst my collection of old papers and books I found a pamphlet about the Church in Burma in which were articles by many interesting people, British and Burmese. These included short accounts about Burma under the Japanese occupation.

It was lucky timing that my brother and his wife visited Burma in Jan/Feb of 2012 and their son Michael in March. It meant that I could include some of their photos. The country was opening up but there was still a sense that they saw what the authorities wanted them to see.

In a previous year when they had planned to go Aung San Suu Kyi had been asking for people not to visit.

As the absorbing task of putting all this together was nearing completion I felt nervous. It was now April 2012 and in Burma the by-elections were approaching, but in the few days leading up to this there was nothing in the news. This feeling was not unlike the one I had had in 2007 – this time it was anticipation but also fear that other news events would be considered of more immediate concern to us in England, fear that this huge milestone in the country's recent history would be ignored and forgotten.

And then reports started to arrive. Aung San Suu Kyi had already been released from her prolonged house arrest on November 13th 2010. (This was 6 days after the result from the General Election on November 7th which the United Nations declared fraudulent.) In April 2012 her party the National League for Democracy announced that she was elected to the Pyithu Hluttaw, the lower house of the Burmese Parliament, representing the constituency of Kawhmu. In this by-election the NLD won 43 of the 45 vacant seats in the lower house. The world saw that journalists were able to record openly what was happening and people were celebrating in the streets.

CONTENTS

Many place names have changed - for the sake of consistency Myanmar is referred to as Burma, and other places are referred to by names mentioned in the diary (chapters 5 and 6) Some place names in China and India have also changed or have alternative spellings.

1
A young Englishwoman arrives in China in 1926

'He is a Mr Pei, about twenty five years old, and one of China's students. He is a Nationalist and his views are most interesting. It is very pathetic though that he is thoroughly pessimistic about China's weakness. He said one day "There are many books written 'How to save China', 'Why China is weak' etc. etc. They are very fine compositions, but they are no use. We cannot carry them out. No one knows how."' Marian

In the 1920' s and 30's two sisters, Marian and Josephine Chapman travelled thousands of miles from their home in England to work in China and Burma as Christian missionaries. In both countries they were to find themselves in the midst of political turmoil followed by the terrors of the Japanese invasion during World War 2.

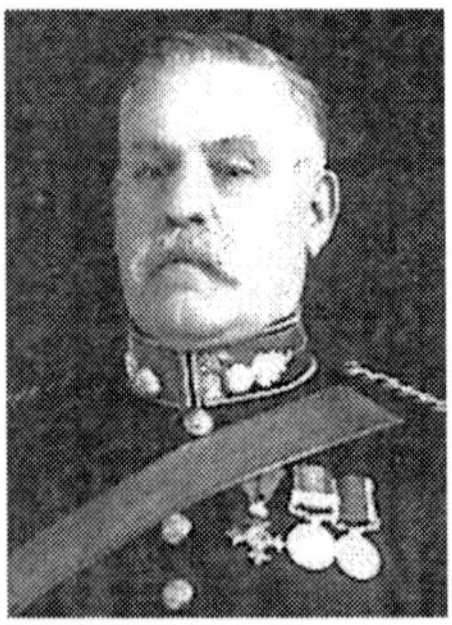

In 1926 Marian arrived in China aged 23. Only two of her letters survive but they reveal many things. She witnessed the civil war in Shanghai which had reached a particularly savage phase in 1927 with communists being rounded up by Chiang Kai-shek's troops and shot in the streets. She also experienced hostility to foreigners- often referred to as 'foreign devils'- and described obstacles preventing her from doing the work she had travelled so far to do.

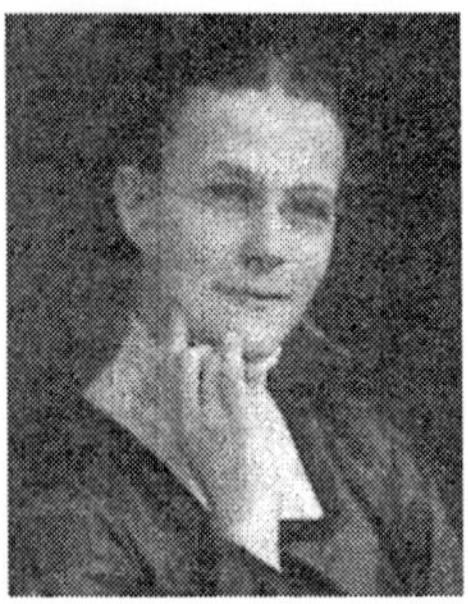

The first letter was written when she had just heard news of her father's death in England. Major Joseph Chapman OBE had been buried with full military honours:

'...following the committal three volleys were fired over the grave, and the sounding of the Last Post by Trumpeters of the R.A. signified that Major Chapman, for 45 years a British soldier under a Queen and two Kings, was at rest.' (extract from Kentish Times, 1927)

Marian and Josephine came from a very large family. Their mother Annie was Joseph's second wife and several older brothers had military careers, including the oldest, Ernest born in 1885, and Melrose who served in the Indian Army. Jo mentioned Melrose in her diary in 1942 when he sent her a coded message which probably saved her life.

When Marian chose to go to China had the family heard about the Boxer Rebellion which had happened only 25 years previously? Christian missionaries and foreigners had been savagely attacked and killed in northern China around Peking (Beijing) and many had in fact left the country. Marian's first surviving letter seems full of anxiety but also hope and the faith that had given her the strength to leave her familiar life in England.

182 Range Road, Shanghai

25. 3.27

Dear Mum and Everybody

Last Sunday the cable about Dad came and I have written two letters to you and sent one by Express mail and one via Siberia, but as the Post Office went on strike last Monday and is still on strike I am afraid those letters are still in Shanghai, though there is the barest possibility that they have been sent. I am sending this by a French boat leaving for England tomorrow. I am waiting anxiously for more news of course we get no letters these days. I still hope you will get the other two letters before you receive this one so I will not say again the things I said in them.

News is black today. Hankow seems to be doing badly. The Consul at Nanking has died of his wounds and rumour has it that worse things are transpiring there. We hope this last is not true. We are expecting that the Settlement will be attacked tonight at the junction of Range Road and Syechwan Road which is part of the boundary between the Settlement and that part of the Chinese city called Chapii, which has already suffered badly through the fighting between N & S though there was remarkably little. Since Monday when Shanghai fell to the South (the Nationalists) the Settlement has been gay with Nationalist flags. I think the Nationalist cause is good, but it is its great weakness that it is so utterly unable to control the Communistic element.

We go on studying Chinese hoping against hope. I have a Chinese teacher for two hours every morning. He is a Mr Pei, about twenty five years old, and one of China's students. He is a Nationalist and his views are most interesting. It is very pathetic though that he is thoroughly pessimistic about China's weakness. He said one day "There are many books written 'How to save China', 'Why China is weak' etc. etc. They are very fine compositions, but they are no use. We cannot carry them out. No one knows how."

Bishop Holden is in Hankow at present. We wish he were safely housed in Shanghai. However 'underneath are the everlasting arms wherever we are and whatever is happening, in England or China or anywhere.'

Monday was a chilling day. Mary and I went out and suddenly I saw a boy on a bicycle with the Nationalist flag in front, he was followed by a whole crowd of others all with flags. High on the topmost point of the Post Office the flag was hoisted and the same thing hung out of every shop window. The street was full of the smoke of crackers. There seems no doubt that the majority of the Chinese in Shanghai had already Southern sympathies and they must have had all those flags safely hidden somewhere waiting for the great day. We are all well and quite safe. My love to all Marian

(Added the following day)

PS The settlement was not attacked last night but some of the Nanking rumours are true. The British Consul has not died but is badly wounded.

The comments made by her tutor, Mr Pei probably refer to several aspects of China's recent history, the weakening and collapse of China's last dynasty, the Qing, and problems during the early years of the new government of the Republic of China which was established in 1912. This replaced the ancient feudal system, but one of its early leaders, Yuan Shih-kai aspired himself to become an emperor. He died in 1916, and there followed a confused period when ancient warlords continued to assert their power in many areas.

Sun Yat-sen(1866-1925) is regarded of the Father of the Republic and had been promoting revolutionary ideas while studying at the Hong Kong College of Medicine for Chinese. He went on to co-found the Kuomintang (Nationalists Party) and with help from the Soviet Union developed the political philosophy known as the Three Principles of the People – nationalism, democracy and the people's livelihood. He was influenced by Western ideas, and when asked by one of the leading generals about the success of the revolution, he said:

"To Christianity more than to any other single cause. Along with its ideals of religious freedom, and along with these it inculcates everywhere a doctrine of universal love and peace. These ideals appeal to the Chinese; they largely caused the Revolution, and they largely determined its peaceful character."

Was Mr Pei also referring to weakness caused by opium addiction which was widespread in China? For centuries opium had been used for medicinal purposes but only by small numbers of wealthy people. The Opium Wars between 1839 and 1860 happened after many disputes between the Qing Dynasty and the British Empire. Britain wanted to adjust the inbalance in trade as they were buying many goods from China such as tea, porcelain and silk for which they were paying in silver.

Chinese laws had been passed to stop the smoking of opium mixed with tobacco – a habit which had been introduced into China by Europeans. The Emperor Dao Guang (1821-1850) ordered that Guangdon (Canton) be closed to opium traffic. Lin Zexu, the High Commissioner to Canton, took steps to stop the trade, and in response the British sent warships and forced the Chinese to sign treaties granting favourable trading rights to foreigners. The territory of Hong Kong became a British Colony.

Lin Zexu wrote a letter to Queen Victoria (it is not known whether she received it) in which he said:

'... so long as you do not take it (opium) yourselves, but continue to make it and tempt the people of China to buy it, you will be showing yourselves careful of your own lives, but careless of the lives of other people, indifferent in your greed for gain to the harm you do to others: such conduct is repugnant to human feelings..'

Was Mr Pei also thinking back to what had happened to the Empire of China? At its height around 1851 it had a huge economy and ruled over 432 million people, more than a third of the world's population. However it kept its ancient and highly valued traditional skills and customs and did not develop industries. It came to be exploited by foreign powers.

During the following years there were a number of rebellions and movements which were driven by contradictory ideas. The Taiping

Rebellion attacked the Qing government and their failure to stand up to Western aggression. It became a widespread civil war in southern China from 1859 – 1864 led by a Christian convert Hong Xiuquan, who believed he was the younger brother of Jesus Christ. His armies controlled millions of people and their social reforms forbade the smoking of opium and included a ban on the ancient and cruel custom of footbinding, a belief in the idea of 'property in common', and the replacing of Confucianism, Buddhism and Chinese folk religion with a form of Christianity.

It was a bloody conflict with many civilians involved and there are reports of millions of deaths with mass executions and the destruction of many cities. It was finally crushed by the Qing government with the eventual aid of French and British forces. However future leaders were to look back on it as an inspiration and an attempt to overthrow a corrupt feudal system.

The Boxer Rebellion (Yihetuan Movement) between 1898 and 1901 was also fuelled by anger about opium and foreign imperialism but in contrast it was against Christianity - the religion so closely associated with foreign powers. *'The Society of Righteous and Harmonious Fists'* came to be known as *'The 'Boxers'* and were a secret society in the northern province of Shandong, which developed from other similar movements, many members of which had lost their livelihoods due to natural disasters and drug addiction. They believed that through martial arts training and prayers they could perform extraordinary and magical feats.

In the Spring of 1900 the Boxer movement spread north towards Peking where in an area south of the Forbidden City there were foreign diplomatic legations belonging to the United Kingdom, France, Germany, Italy, Austria-Hungary, Spain, Belgium, the Netherlands, the United States, Russia and Japan. Foreign legations existed in many Chinese cities and had instituted treaties which gave them special trading privileges, territorial rights and immunities from Chinese Law, they controlled customs and postal services, seized revenues and owned industries.

The Boxer Rebels marched on Peking and the Empress Dowager Cixi reluctantly supported them, though officials were divided in their reactions. The eight nation alliance of foreign powers sent for armed troops and warships.

A Chinese official at the time said:

"Take away your missionaries and your opium and you will be welcome."

Continuing disagreements about whether or not to support the Boxer Movement weakened the Qing Government, there were traditionalists who wanted to remove foreigners and moderates who advocated diplomacy. During discussions the Empress Dowager Cixi said :

"Perhaps their magic (the Boxers) is not to be relied upon; but can we not rely on the hearts and minds of the people? Today China is extremely weak. We have only the people's hearts and minds to depend upon. If we cast them aside and lose the people's hearts, what can we use to sustain the country?"

There was much confusion and attacks on foreign legations. Many foreign civilians, missionaries and businessmen took refuge in the British legation and surrounding buildings. In June the Empress Dowager declared war against all foreign powers, but some regional governors withheld knowledge of this from many of the population, and some entered into negotiations with foreign powers to keep their own armies out of the conflict. Cixi is reported to have said to the Grand Council:

"Now they (the Powers) have started the aggression, and the extinction of our nation is imminent. If we just fold our arms and yield to them, I would have no face to see our ancestors after death. If we must perish, why not fight to the death?" (The reference to ancestors is an aspect of Confucianism – an ethical system developed from the teachings of the Chinese philosopher – where filial piety must be shown to the living and the dead, so ancestors were held in high respect)

Cixi began to blockade the legations with the Peking Armies. She also said,

"I have always been of the opinion that the allied armies had been permitted to escape too easily in 1860. Only a united effort was then necessary to have given China the victory. Today, at last, the opportunity for revenge has come."

Many Protestant, Catholic and Russian Orthodox missionaries and their Chinese converts were massacred throughout northern China by the Boxers and government troops, who also burned down churches. The Rebellion was ultimately suppressed by the eight foreign powers, the largest of which was the Japanese. There followed chaos and destruction. It was a period of very hot weather, with temperatures sometimes reaching 110 degrees F. A foreign journalist, George Lynch said,

"...there are things that I must not write, and that may not be printed in England, which would seem to show that this Western civilization of ours is merely a veneer over savagery."

Several months after the Boxer Rebellion and heavily disguised, the Empress Dowager fled from Peking to Shaanxi province where she took refuge in an area of steep mountain passes. There followed a confused period – there is an old Chinese saying:

"The people are afraid of officials, the officials are afraid of foreigners, and the foreigners are afraid of the people.'.

The situation within the Qing Dynasty was also unclear, as the Empress Dowager Cixi had placed the Guangxu Emperor under house arrest where he remained until his death in 1908 (strangely on the same day as Cixi's) – she had by this time appointed the new Emperor, a tiny boy who grew up imprisoned in the Forbidden City during the beginnings of the new Republican Government .

Looking back, many different views are expressed about the Boxer Rebellion. Some Chinese saw the Boxers as superstitious and 'uncivilized'. Sun Yat-sen called them 'bandits' but as time wore on he came to praise them for fighting foreign imperialism, being courageous and fearless unto death. The Russian writer Leo Tolstoy also praised them and was harshly critical of the behaviour of Russian and Western troops in China and what he called 'Christian brutality'. There is debate as to whether it was an anti-imperialist movement, whether the predominantly peasant rebels were concerned with regional issues, or whether it was mainly a religious war.

In the 1920's there was another movement called *'The May Fourth Movement for a New Culture'* which attacked all religions including

Confucianism and Buddhism as well as Christianity, regarding them as superstitions. It promoted science and an easier form of Chinese writing. A colleague of Sun Yat-sen, Zhu Zhixin (1885-1920) had published an article *'What is Jesus'*, where he argued that Jesus was an ordinary illegitimate peasant child no different from similar individuals in Chinese history who had led bands of mystical enthusiasts. A student movement was founded to counteract what was seen as the influence of Christianity against China's attempts to make reforms. There were publications and rallies up to around 1927, and Christian schools were required to have Chinese leadership.

2
Civil war and refuge in Cheung Chow Island in 1928

"Do you think that we, a nation with 4,000 years, will disappear in such a short period as a century?" Chang Hsueh-liang in 1935

The Chinese Communist Party (CCP) also came into being around this time, inspired by ideas of Lenin and Karl Marx and with Mao Tse-Tung as an early member, and to begin with it worked together with the Kuomintang. However Mao became disillusioned with the corruption of the Kuomintang and the continuing powers of the feudal warlords. Members were recruited to the CCP from the many workers who suffered harsh working conditions where child labour was common and there were huge number of farmers struggling to survive in the countryside.

During these years the CCP went through different phases, at times it was harsh and uncompromising, destroying religious symbols such as Buddhas and questioning traditional Chinese ideas within families, however during persecution by Nationalist armies it went underground and became more moderate, giving people hope for a better future than they were experiencing under the new Nationalist Government.

It was after Sun Yat-sen's death in 1925 that one of his followers Chiang Kai-shek seized control of the Kuomintang and in 1926-27 brought most of south and central China under his control with a military campaign. Around the time of Marian's first letter Communists were being savagely eliminated, there was the April 12 Incident in Shanghai and similar mass killings in other cities such as Guangzhou and Changsha.

In another letter she wrote in 1928 to one of her sisters she described the hostility she was experiencing. Now she was living in Cheung Chow Island, near Hong Kong. It begins with an explanation:

6 Cheung Chow Island, Hong Kong

13.2.28 '... I do write home regularly every week and have only missed once since I left which was last week when I took my second exam (which I have passed) and the home letters are meant for everybody....... my time really is full. .'

There are difficulties she could not have forseen before she left England and she appears to abandon efforts to explain problems about having time to write and getting letters home.

'Yes I did promise to send you some curios and I have not forgotten, but living in Shanghai and Hong Kong on a salary intended for up country where living is much cheaper makes it impossible to do these extras which one would otherwise very gladly do. In Shanghai things were so expensive that the cheapest decent lodging I could get for sometime took more than the allowance we get up country so the society had to allow me and others in the same predicament a rise of salary for a time. Down here we are just able to manage on the ordinary allowance but we have nothing over. I'm sorry, but when we get up country again and the financial state of things is easier I will get some curios and things.

You say you wonder if the work is what I thought it would be. I have seen very little of it so far. I was only six weeks in Hankow (a city inland which later in the war became a political and military centre when eastern cities had been taken by the Japanese) *for at that time the anti foreign feeling was so strong that very little work could be done. Down here the work is very much more in institutions than it is up country, the pastoral and evangelistic work in these big ports is done much more by the Chinese Church itself because things are much more advanced. But from the little I have seen and from what I have heard it is about what I thought only naturally in England I could not really see all the difficulties. It is certainly harder than I thought. But I shall be happy in it. At present I am doing language, language, language.*

Your photo is very good. Many thanks for it. My photo gallery is gradually improving.I had written to Miss Sands for Christmas before your letter arrived telling me about her. I am sorry she was hurt. I have probably hurt several people by not writing last year. My correspondence, except letters home fared badly because well for several reasons. I am sorry she was hurt...... This island is very beautiful. I am sharing a little house with Miss Law. We are both doing language and have a teacher here. The island is about five miles round and everywhere around are mountain islands in the sea. On clear nights the lights of Hong Kong are very easily seen. I like it umpteen times better than Shanghai. But you will have heard all this from my home letters. Cheerio, and goodbye for the present. I hope you are very well

Your loving Marian

Cheung Chow Island lies to the west of Hong Kong and with its narrow streets, fishing boats and peaceful sandy beaches it must have been a welcome refuge after the dangers she had experienced in Shanghai. People came to this area to get away from the prolonged Chinese Civil war.

Marian must have travelled to England for a holiday as her name appears on the passenger list of a ship leaving London in October 1931 and bound for Yokohama via Hong Kong and Shanghai. This was the RMS Corfu, a Royal Mail Ship and ocean liner operated by the Peninsular and Oriental Steam Navigation Company, built in Glasgow and later converted for use as an armed merchant cruiser during World War 2.

When she arrived back in China it is difficult to know how much she would have been able to hear and read about what was happening in such a vast country. The Civil war she had witnessed between the Nationalists and Communists was continuing in many areas. In addition to this, military incidents between Japan and China had been going on for many years.

Chang Hsueh-liang (1901 – 2001) was a significant figure at this time (perhaps this is her writing on an old newspaper cutting of him standing next to Chiang Kai-shek?) After the assassination of his father by the Japanese in 1928 he became the strongest warlord in Manchuria in northern China with massive armies, and later that year he proclaimed his loyalty to the Kuomintang. In 1931 Japan invaded Manchuria, an area of rich natural resources, and occupied it until the end of World War 2. When attacked Chang Hsueh-liang withdrew his forces and put them at the disposal of Chiang Kai-shek.

In 1933 Japan defied world opinion and withdrew from the League of Nations. This was after the Mukden Incident, when part of a railway Japan had built was blown up, with conflicting reports about who was responsible. China appealed to the League of Nations who ordered the Japanese Government to stop the invasion of Manchuria. Representatives from many nations were stunned as Yosuke Matsuoka, dressed in black, and other Japanese delegates walked from the hall. "*We are not coming back,*" he said.

The 42 other countries had voted unanimously that Japan should withdraw her troops from Manchuria and restore the territory to Chinese sovereignty. Matsuoka's speech was being translated, and he had shouted from the rostrum –

"Japan will oppose any attempt at international control of Manchuria. It does not mean that we defy you, because Manchuria belongs to us by right....Read your history. We recovered Manchuria from Russia. We made it what it is today....We look into the gloom of the future and can see no certain gleam of light before us."

He stated that Manchuria was a matter of life and death for Japan and that no compromise was possible:

' *"Japan has been and will always be the mainstay of peace, order and progress in the Far East."*

When international control of Machuria was suggested he asked,

"Would the American people agree to such control of the Panama Canal Zone; would the British permit it over Egypt?....The Japanese people will oppose any such attempt in Manchuria. I beg of this body to realize the facts and see a vision of the future. I earnestly beg of you to deal with us on our terms, to give us your confidence. To deny us this appeal will be a mistake. I ask you not to adopt this report."

He also said: *"It is a source of profound regret and disappointment to the Japanese government that the draft report has now been adopted by this assembly. Japan has been a member of the League since its inception. Our delegates in past conferences participated in the drafting of the League covenant"..... "We have been proud to be members, associated with the leading nations of the world in one of the grandest purposes in which humanity could unite.....*

".....It is a matter of common knowledge that Japan's policy is fundamentally inspired by the genuine desire to guarantee peace in the Far East and to contribute to the maintenance of peace throughout the world. ....I need hardly add that the Japanese government will persist in their desire to contribute to human welfare, and will continue their policy of co-operating in all sincerity in the work dedicated to world peace.".

During its occupation of Manchuria Japan used forced Chinese labour and there were many atrocities inflicted on civilians.

Despite periods of opium addiction and travels abroad in Britain and Europe, Chang Hsueh-liang was nicknamed 'China's Napoleon' and also 'the Young Marshall' and worked with Chiang Kai-shek against the

Communists whose armies were eventually forced to flee for their lives. In 1934 they walked 6,000 miles to China's desolate northwest country, crossing deep gorges, mountain ranges and swamps and establishing a guerrilla base at Yan'an in Shaanxi Province. Many thousands died during what was known as *'The Long March'.* Though small in number after this exhausting and terrifying journey, the survivors grew in strength and reorganized themselves under Mao Tse-tung.

Perhaps Marian saw a copy of an interview the journalist Gareth Jones had with Chang Hsueh-liang in Hankow on June 20th 1935. It gives a glimpse of the plans the Nationalists had at that time and their attitude to the Communists, and when asked about Japan Chang declines to answer.

Gareth Jones – *"The anti-Communist fights have been a great success and have been applauded."*

Marshall – *"The Communists are bandits. We have broken the main body. Some of them remain in bandit gangs scattered here and there. We have put 7000 Communists into reformation. They are however very desperate for they fight for their lives. They are afraid of returning to their villages for there the villagers who know them would kill them. Thus we have to settle them far away. Our grip over Szechuan will increase as time goes on. Not only have we our military force there, but also they are spreading their ideas of unification. In Kivenchow and Yunnan it is the same."*

Jones – *"In Canton there is opposition to unification. Will the building of roads and the Hankow and Canton railway be a help to unification?"*

Marshall – *"Yes, it will mean the spread of ideas also, and a cultural link with the south."*

Jones – *"What means have you in mind to extend the grip of the Central Government to Szechuan?"*

Marshall – *"We are going to build a railway south of the Yangtze, through Changsha to Kweichow and then up to Szechuan. We are going to build motor roads."*

Jones – *"What are you doing that the south shall be military minded? I was in Changsha and the youngsters said that they wished to enter military institutes in order to fight Japan."*

(This tickled the Marshall and he seemed pleased.) *"We believe in stress upon military training in order to strengthen the character of the young Chinese in general education."*

Jones – *"Has the Japanese aggression made any change in the policy of Central Government, ie of co-operation towards the Japanese?"*

(Obviously a brick, rather embarrassed Marshall replies coldly in Chinese and Consul translates) *"I could reply, but that is a question on which I would rather not speak."* (Silence, then laughter.)

Jones – *"Has the Nanking Government any plans for state industry? In every country in the Far East I have seen advances of State Socialism."*

Marshall – *"We have the National Economic Council which is going to consider plans for new industries, including State Industries."*

Jones – *"Do you lay great stress on aviation?"*

Marshall – *"Yes, there will be a new route to Szechuan. My second son is going to be an aviator and is exceedingly keen and will have long years of training. I have my own aeroplane and I am keen on flying.(Ford Monoplane)"*

Jones - *"Mr Matsuoka said that China would in this century be filled either with Bolshevism from Russia or with the spirit of Japonism. What do you think of that?"*

Marshall – (with scorn) – *"Do you think that we, a nation with 4,000 years, will disappear in such a short period as a century?."*

During the year following this interview Chang Hsueh-liang felt driven to take drastic action and kidnapped Chiang Kai-shek, saying he wanted to persuade him to join with the Communists to resist the Japanese invasion. This was known as the Xi'an Incident, and is regarded as a decisive moment in Chinese history. Chiang Kai-shek agreed to unite with the Communists but it only worked for a limited period of time. Chang was imprisoned and then freed after a fortnight, but was later sentenced to 10 years in prison, and when Chiang and his government lost the civil war in 1949 and fled to Taiwan they took Chang with them and kept him under house arrest for 53 years, making him the world's longest held political prisoner. He spent much time reading the bible and doing historical research, and died in 2001 aged 101.

Under the Nationalist government there was much construction of new industry, they sought to keep ancient virtues and adopt modern technology. But life was still very hard for many workers, including children, and the Communist movement went underground and continually sought to recruit new members to its cause.

There was an expansion of missionary activity following the beginnings of the Republic of China. The first medical college for women in China was founded by Dr Mary H Fulton in Guangzhou, and most students became Christians. Other colleges and hospitals were built, with growth of the church in the Lisu tribes of Yunnan.

It sounds as if Marian wrote regular letters home but none others survive, however old photos suggest she was finally able to do some work, and a story of love was beginning to unfold.

3
1937 – A pretty wedding and the prolonged and bloody attack on Shanghai

'...She wore oyster coloured satin....with shoes of the same colour. Her silk net veil was held in place with orange blossoms which were brought from England...' - the Shanghai Times, April 11 1937

In 1934 the Nationalist party started *The New Life Movement* which combined traditional Confucianism, Western Christianity, nationalism and authoritarianism and opposed communism. However it is suggested that these ideals were only meaningful to comparatively small numbers of more affluent Chinese in developed urban areas, and the tens of thousands who were suffering harsh and difficult lives were preoccupied with their daily struggles to survive.

Manchuria was occupied and neither Japan nor China had formally declared war. Japan wanted to avoid the intervention of other countries, particularly Britain and the U S while it sought to acquire territory and access to natural resources. In fact, four years before the attack on the American base at Pearl Harbour it is surprising to realise that Japan was still using military equipment and planes supplied by the U S. Through the 1930's 80% of Japan's oil imports were from the U S, but America disapproved of the expansion of the Japanese Empire and in 1940 passed the Export Control Act which cut oil, iron and steel exports to Japan.

In July 1941 a full embargo was imposed and the U S and Britain began sending supplies to support Chiang Kai-shek's war effort against the Japanese. By that time the defence of China was to be considered vital to the defence of the U S. Amongst Chiang's supporters were powerful drug barons and there were millions of opium addicts in the country. During the Japanese invasion and occupation (1937-45) drug trading also went on between the Japanese and the Chinese. And at that time there were huge fields of red, pink and white poppies in China itself, in the foothill districts of Sichuan province.

Foreign powers were still present in China. The Settlement to which Marian referred in her first letter was an area in Shanghai originally built and and dominated by the British from 1842. Other foreign powers such as the Americans and French, Danes, Germans and

Japanese had also established themselves - the area always remained Chinese sovereign territory but had its own administration and trading privileges. In December 1941 on the same day as Pearl Harbour Japanese troops were to take it by force.

In the 1930's Shanghai was one of the largest cities in the world and a busy cosmopolitan port. White Russians had fled there after the 1917 Revolution and for a time Jews from Europe were able take refuge there. It was a big financial centre and became known as 'The Paris of the East, the New York of the West', electricity and trams were introduced and it had an image that was distinct from all other Chinese cities.

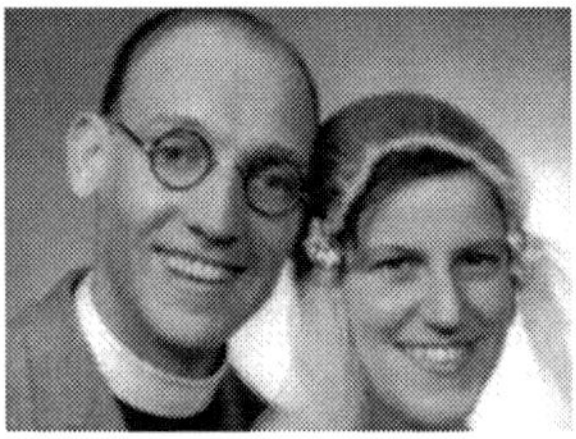

'A pretty wedding took place at 3.30 o'clock yesterday afternoon ....when Miss Marian Elizabeth Chapman, daughter of the late Major J T Chapman O.B.E. and Mrs Chapman of London became the bride of the Rev. Joseph Leach M.A..... She wore oyster coloured satin....with shoes of the same colour. Her silk net veil was held in place with orange blossoms which were brought from England...' (extract from the Shanghai Times, April 11 1937)

This wedding took place at Shanghai cathedral about 4 months before the very dreadful and prolonged Battle of Shanghai. Because of fierce and sustained resistance by the Chinese National Army the Japanese were forced to commit over 200,000 troops, naval vessels and aircraft in order to capture the city. In September 1937 after Shanghai was occupied there is a quote from the Oriental Economist newspaper:

'Japan faces the most critical situation since the Empire's foundation.'

Meanwhile the Chinese government were taking steps to preserve industries under attack. The National Resources Commission began moving industries away from the vulnerable coastal area around Shanghai to remote regions inland. Campaigns for Japanese control of other places continued with mixed results and Chiang Kai-shek refused to negotiate with the Japanese. Air raids on Chinese cities intensified, large battles developed and Peking and Tianjin were taken by Japanese forces. By the end of 1937 Japan held the city of Nanking and Northern

Shaanxi, and the brutality and horror of these campaigns is well known.

Athough well equipped the Japanese forces had a huge task to occupy and control vast areas of the countryside and Chinese guerrilla warfare disrupted their progress in many places. In 1938 Chiang Kai-shek opened dikes on the Yellow River and waters flooded into Henan, Anhui and Jiangsu, destroying villages and drowning thousands of people with many more made homeless. There are different reports of the number of deaths that resulted from this action and the doubtful effect that the flood had on the progress of the Japanese advance.

There were frequent air attacks by high and fast flying Japanese planes. One way civilians learnt to save themselves was to leave built up areas for the safety of the fields during daylight hours and return at night. There were patriotic propaganda posters in the streets of cities and the display of portraits of Chiang Kai-shek and Sun Yat-sen. Anti Japanese propaganda was printed on leaflets which were left where the troops might find them.

There was suffering and disruption on an enormous scale, with displaced civilians fleeing from one place to another, people of all classes struggling to travel by whatever means they could on crowded trains, bicycles, carts, rickshaws and donkeys, with thousands of Chinese soldiers walking from one place to another, many wounded and starving.

It is not known where Marian and her new husband went after their wedding in Shanghai, whether they were there when the city was under attack or had gone somewhere safer. However they did not stay anywhere for long as their children were born in three different places. Looking back over more than 70 years John, their second child writes:

'Tom was born in January 1938 in Lingling, Yungchow in Hunan Province.'

Hunan Province was where Mao Tse-tung had been born into a peasant family in 1893. Four rivers flow into the great Yangtze and the very large Lake Dongting lies in the plains and fertile valleys which are ringed to the east, south and west with mountains.
John writes:

'... and I was born in Hong Kong a couple of years later at the 'Matilda Hospital.'

A year after this in December 1941 Hong Kong was invaded by the Japanese and occupied until August 1945. Anne, their third child was born in 1942 in Gweilin south west of Lingling in Kwangsi Province which is adjacent to Hunan Province. It was from here in 1943 that the family were going to feel under threat from the Japanese and had to try and get back to England by whatever means they could.

An old newspaper cutting with Chang Hsueh-liang *'the Young Marshall'* and Chiang Kai-shek

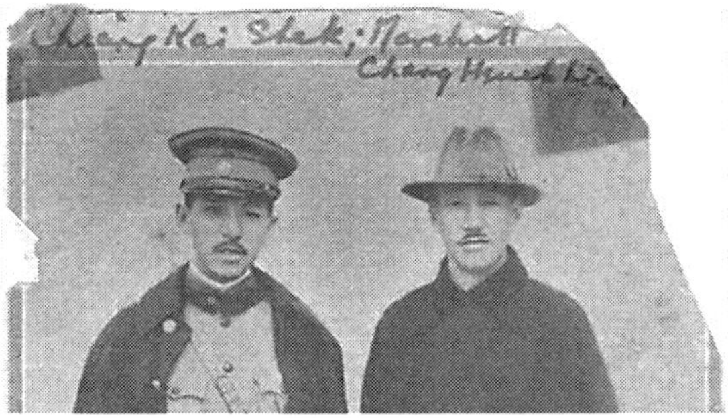

On this old photo is written: *'Our Christmas feast at St John's Church'.* Marian's husband Joe is standing in the centre.

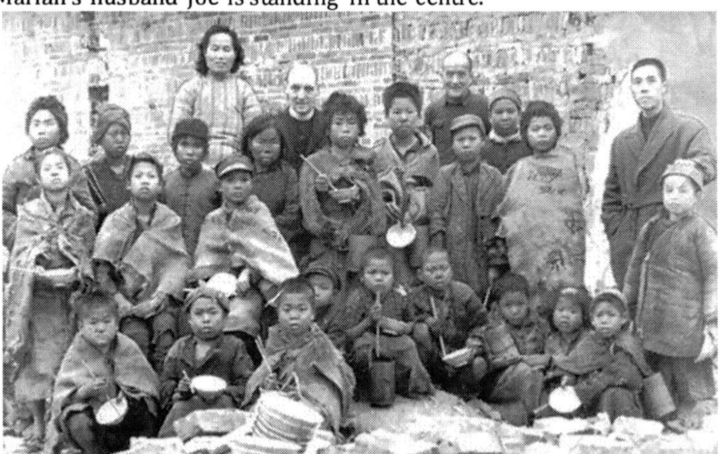

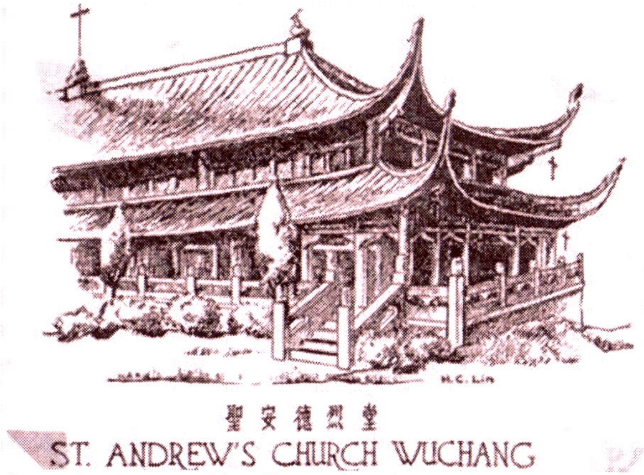

On this photo is written *'A village church in Kwangsi. Tong-Pao-san, a village in the Hingan Parish. The building on the left is the school, and next it is the entrance to the Church. The schoolboys are on the left, some of the local Christians on the right, and in the foreground are, from left to right the Evangelist, the Schoolmaster, the School-master's wife, and the Evangelist's wife....'*

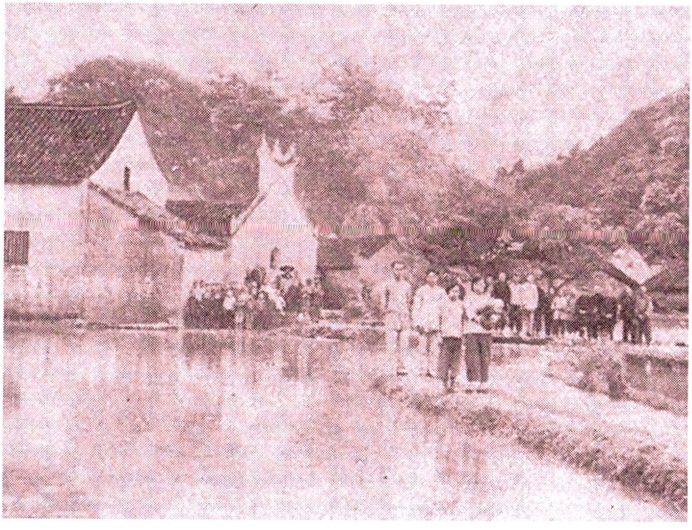

4
Burma

'Worship on the terraces of the Shwedagon Pagoda, Rangoon'

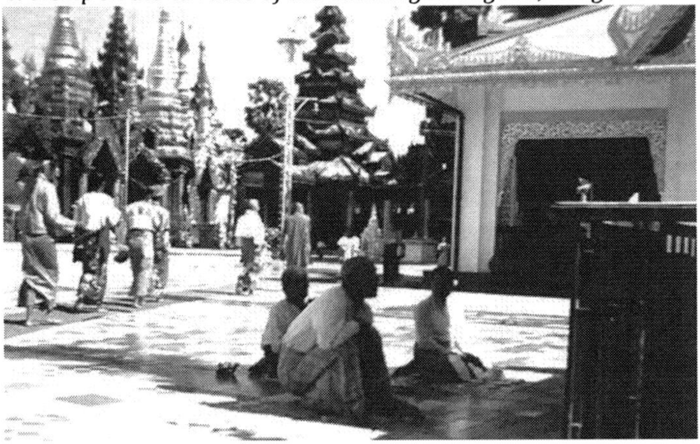

Large Buddha at Prome

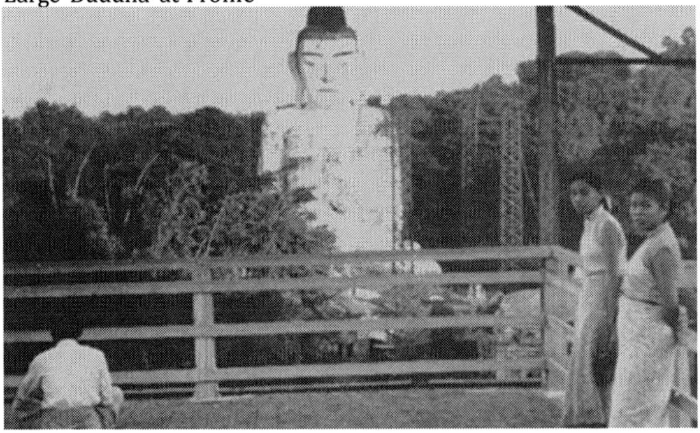

Prome

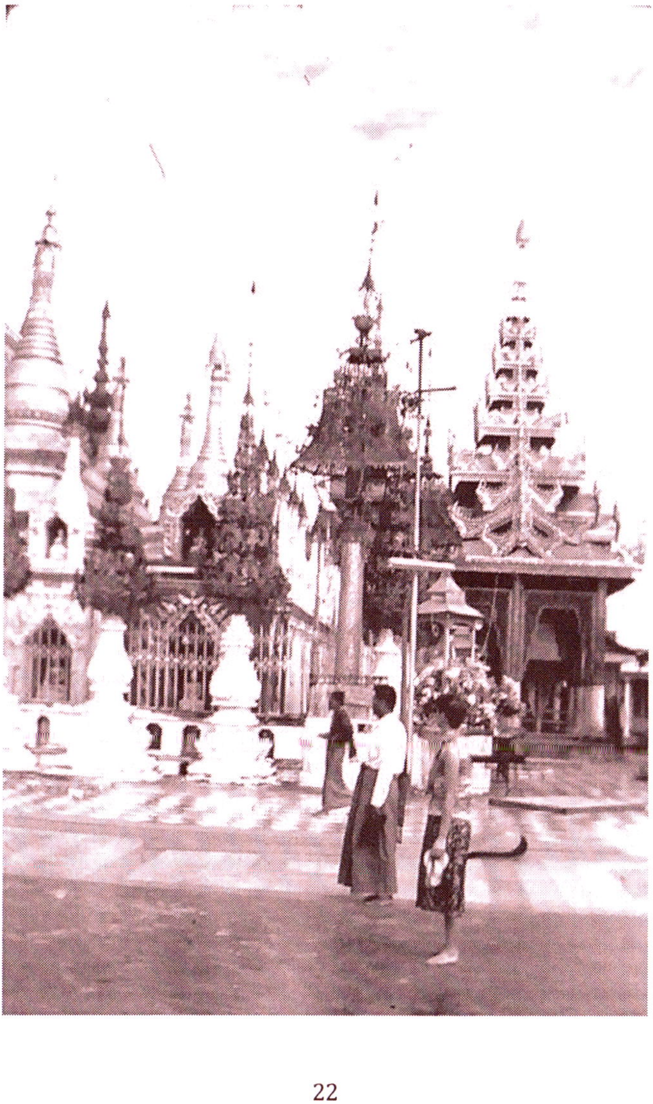

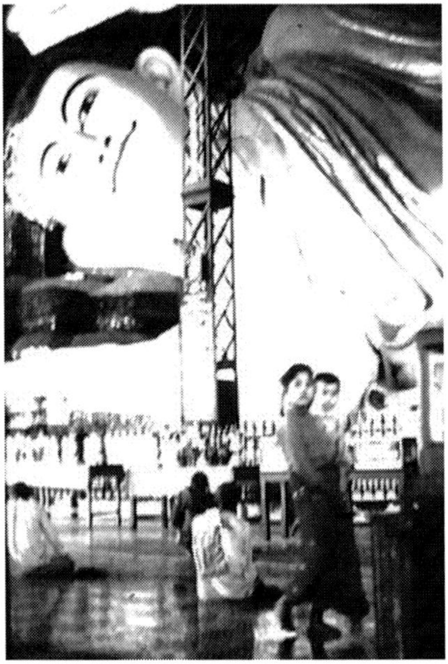

The Shwethalyaung Buddha at Pegu is 117 feet high and was constructed in the 10th century.

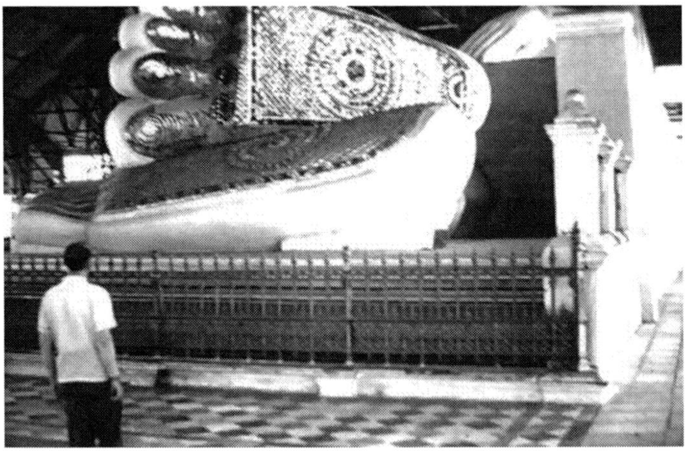

'Shinbyu' is the ceremony when the young boy is robed in rich garments and jewels and rides to the monastery where he is prepared to start his Buddhist life by putting on the simple clothes of a monk.

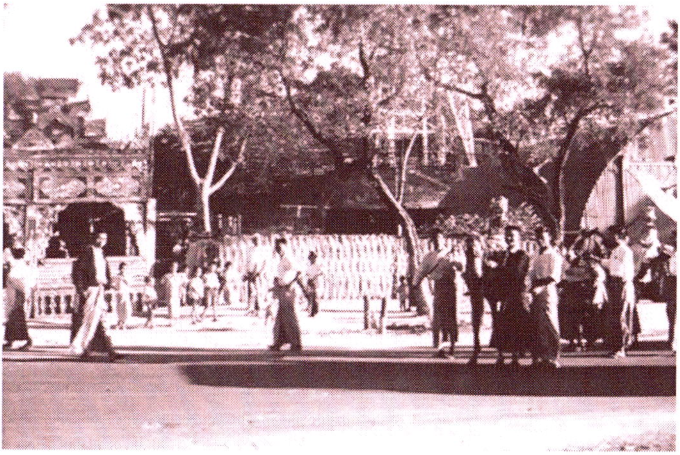

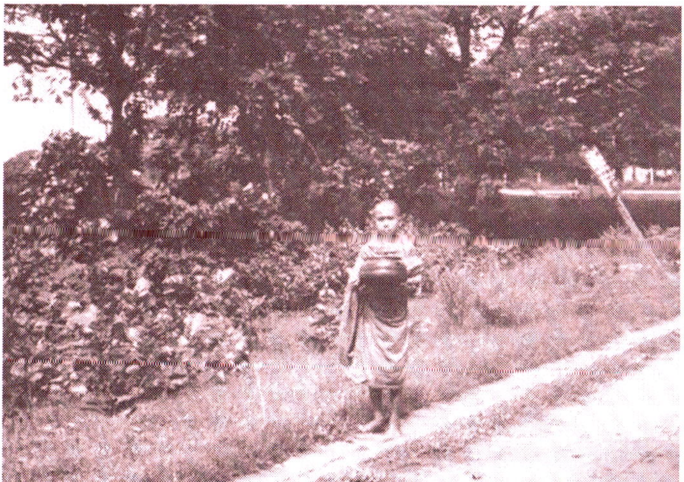

Buddhist nuns

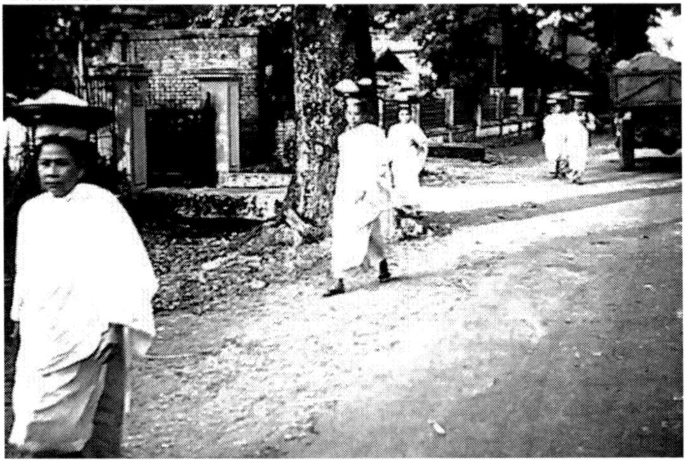

Ladies at Myitkyina

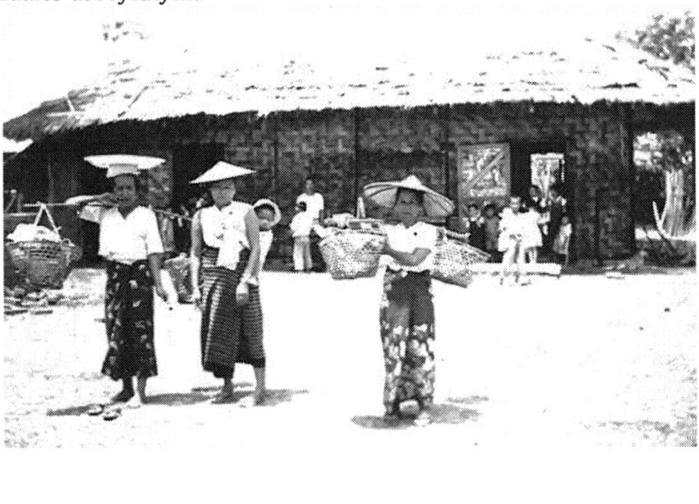

Preparing for market in Mandalay

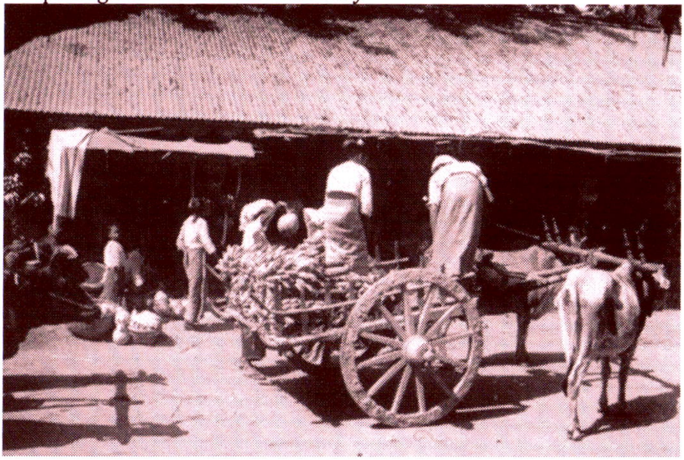

'Floating market'

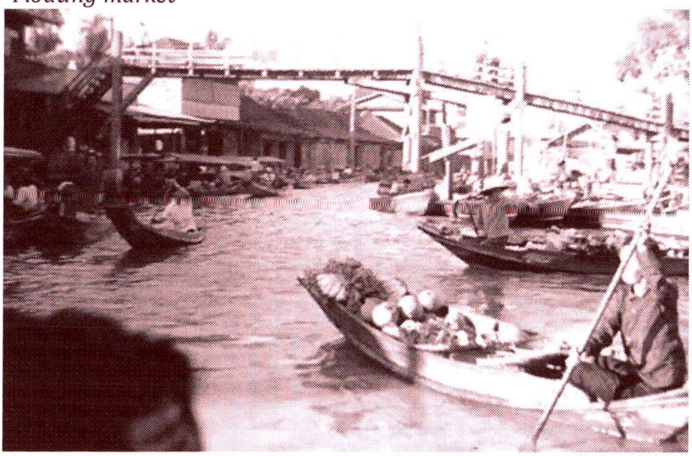

'Houses in the Delta'

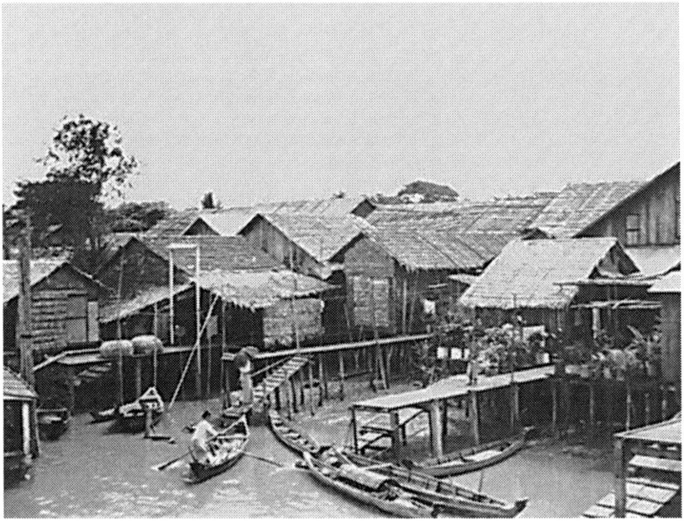

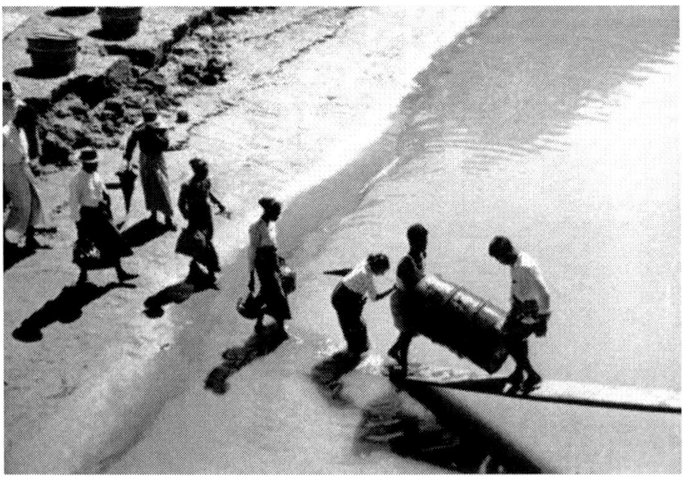

'By the Irrawaddy near Mandalay 1937'

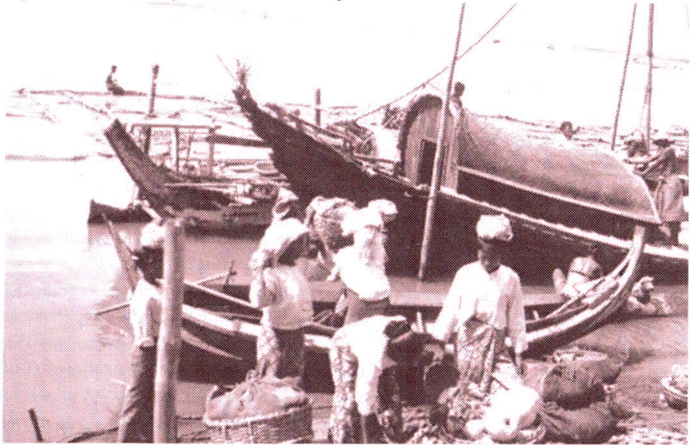

Paddy fields

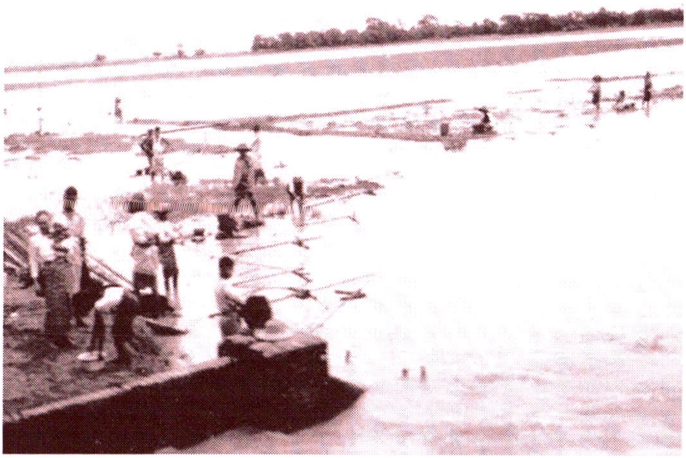

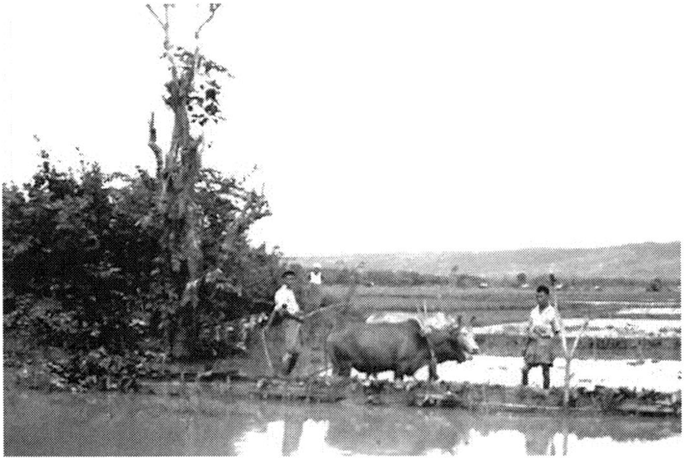

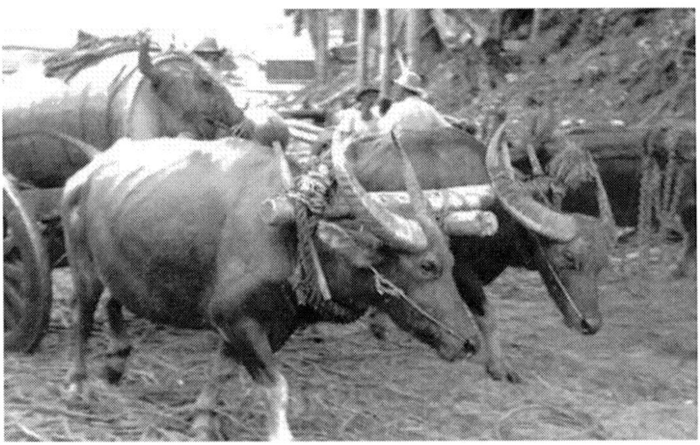

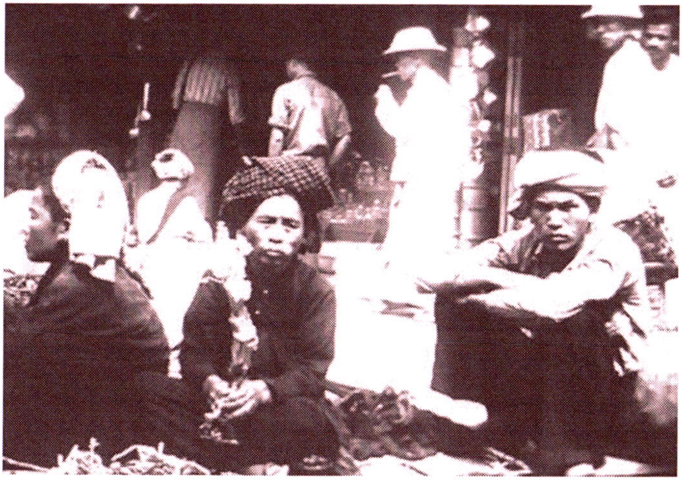

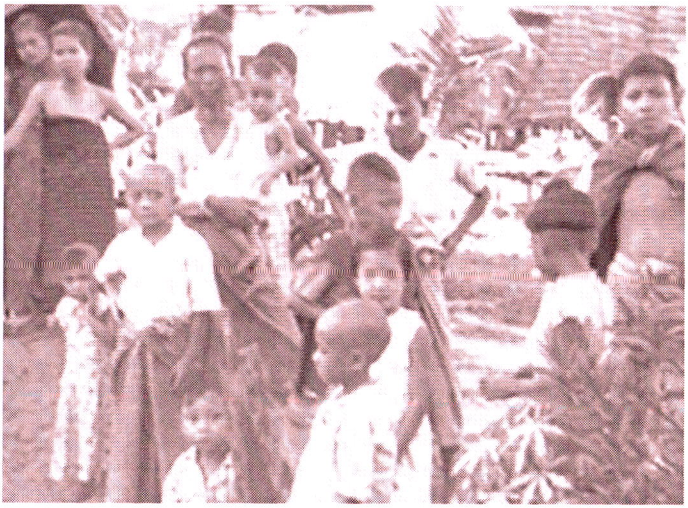

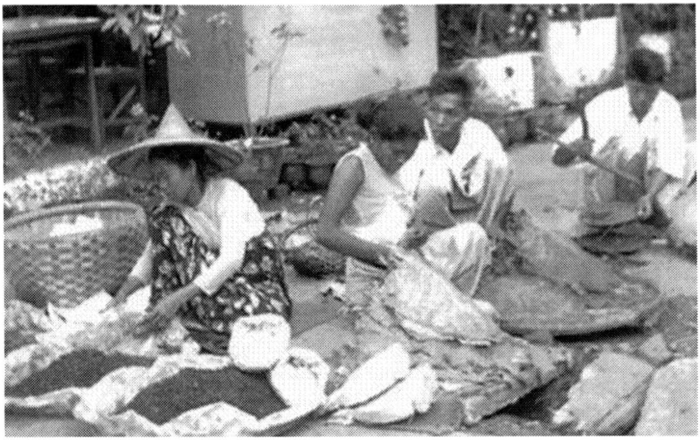

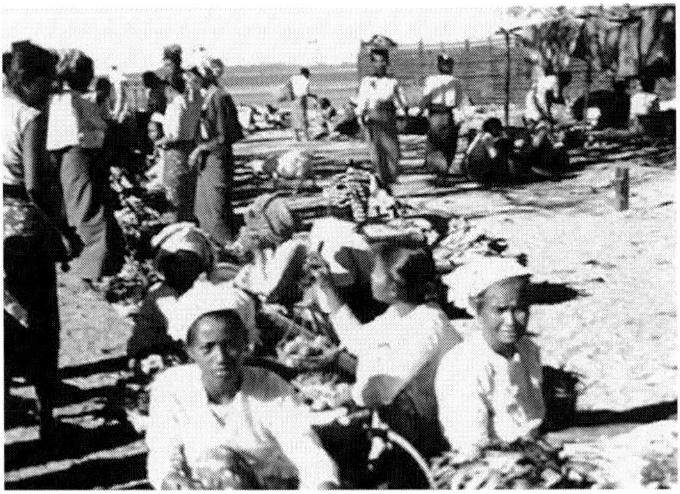

A Christian group

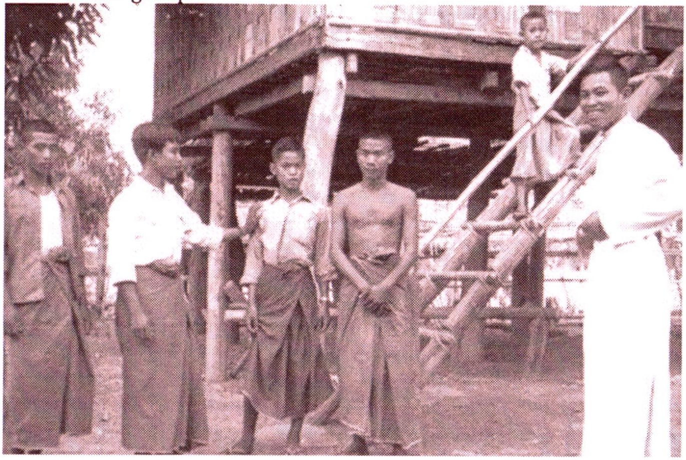

School at Shwebo built by the British

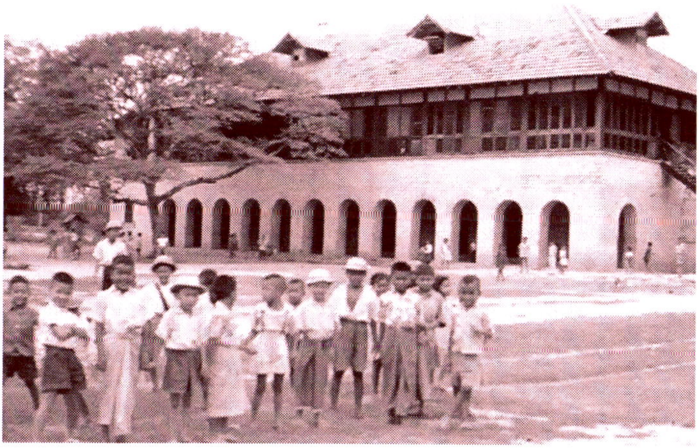

Church at Pa-an

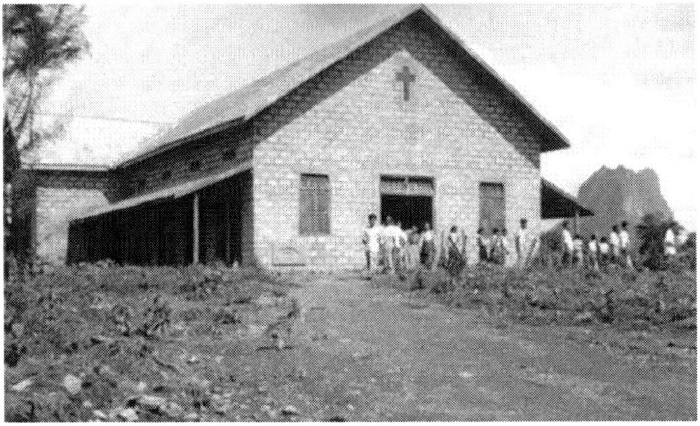

Inside the church

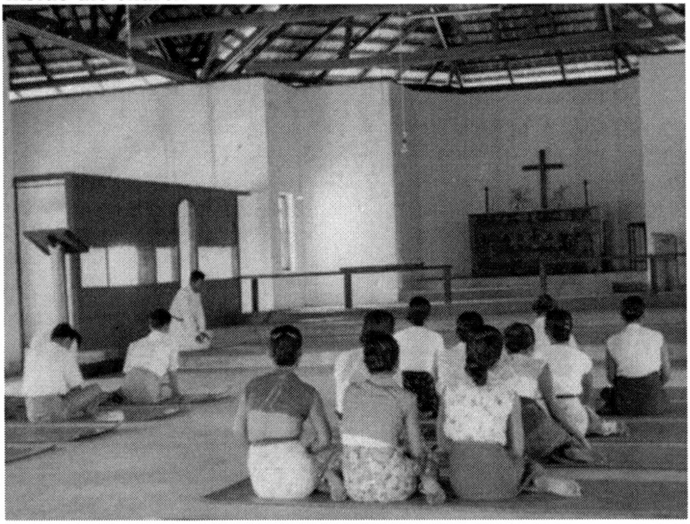

'Approaching Khumi Chin village by boat'

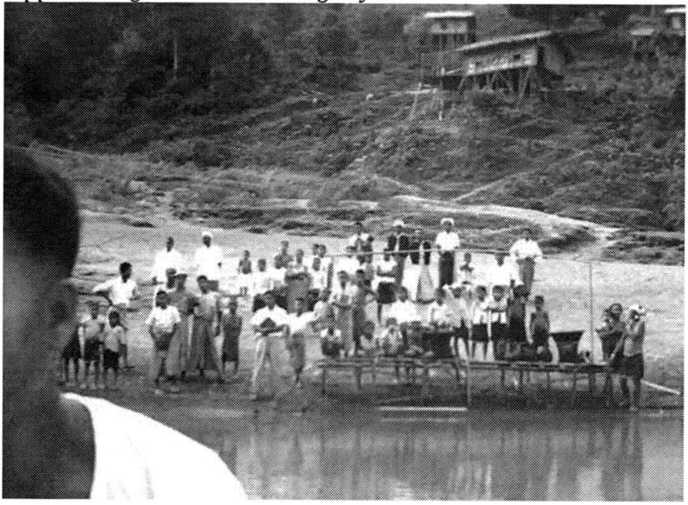

'coming out of church'

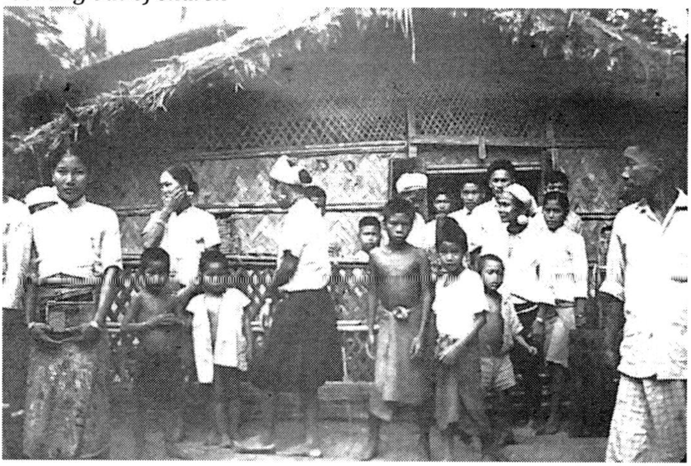

A village scene

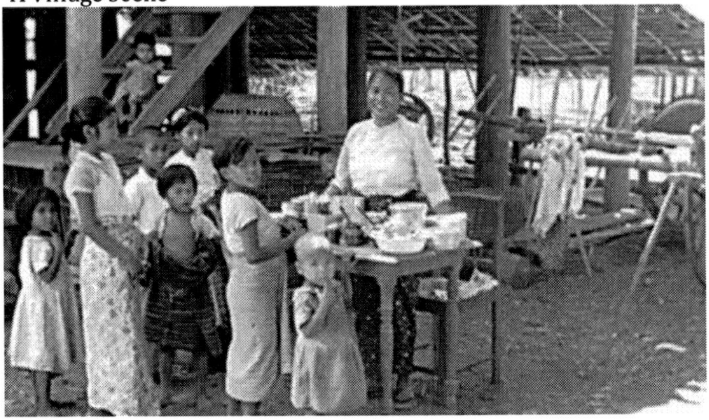

A wooden church

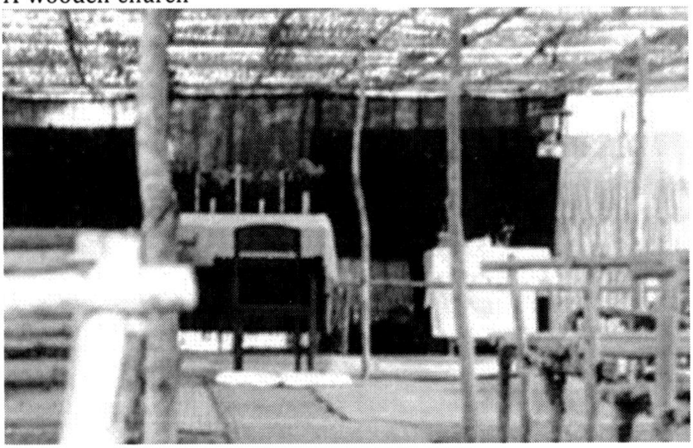

'Tea pickers' - Dorothy Lewis is in the white dress

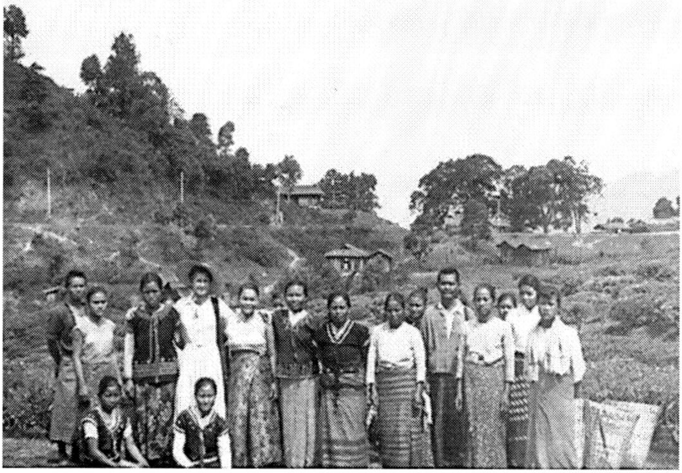

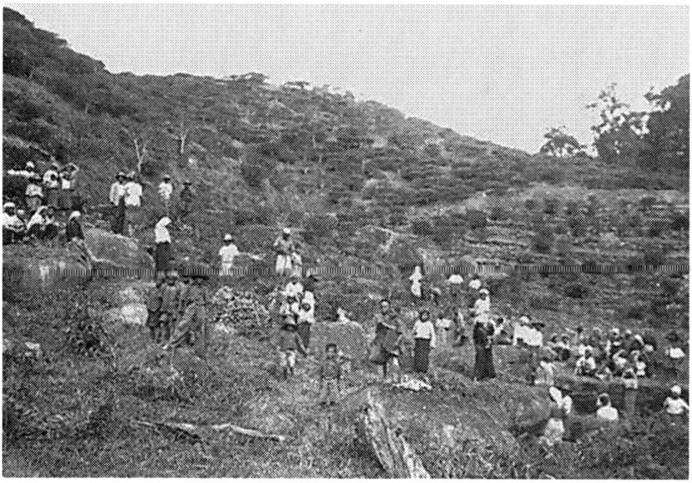

Logs of teak near Mandalay

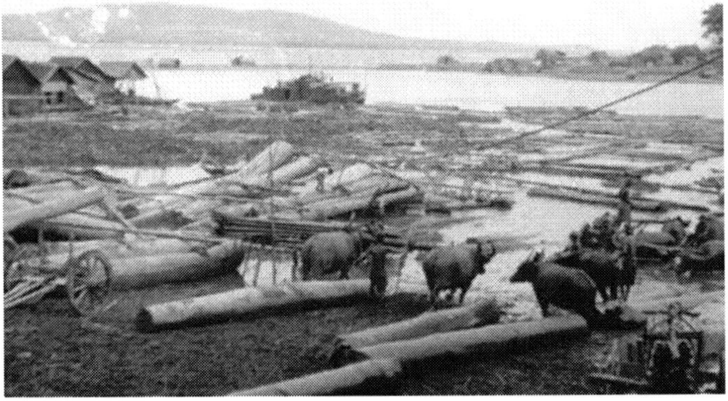

Old ruby mine at Mogok

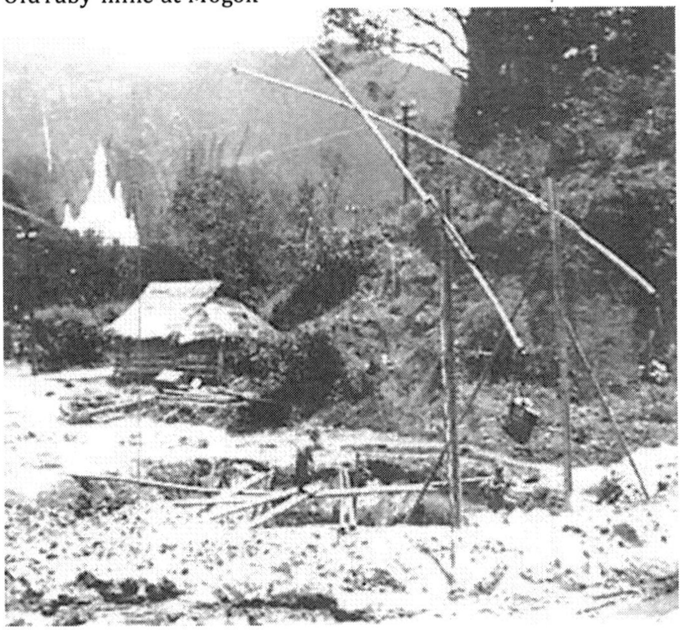

Scene by a river

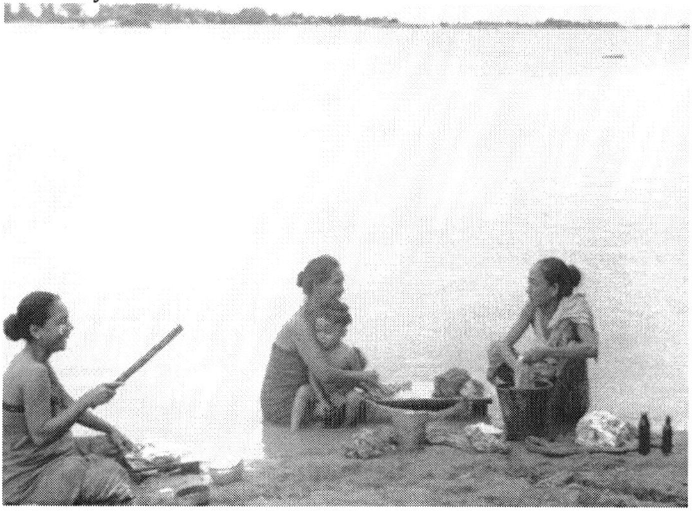

Distant view of the Shwedagon Pagoda

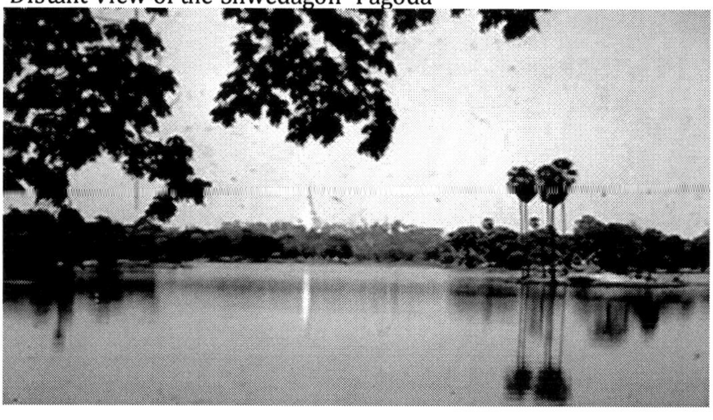

Rangoon

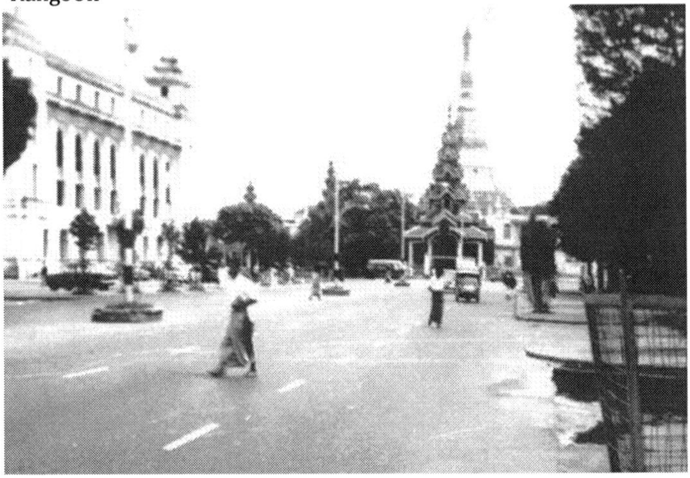

Burma is a very large country with many huge mountain ranges running southwards from the Himalayas. For centuries trading routes between India and China passed through the country and the valuable logs of teak were exported for many uses including European shipbuilding. There are fertile plains and much traffic moved on the many waterways including the famous Irrawaddy which flows south for 1300 miles.

There were ill defined borders with India. King Bodawpaya and King Bagyidaw were faced with rebellions across the border and this resulted in the First Anglo-Burmese War from 1824–1826. This was the most expensive war in the history of British India, followed by the Second and Third Anglo-Burmese Wars which ended in 1885.

It is incredible to read of how the British arrived in Rangoon in1852 and drove the Burmese out of the Shwedagon Pagoda which they then occupied for many years. During this time they carried out acts of sheer vandalism for their own purposes. Burma was one of the most literate states in Asia under the Toungoo Kings and the Konbaung Dynasty. But it was a time of great savagery at the court.

There is an old letter our father Christopher Lewis wrote during a time when he worked in Mandalay, (the date of which is unknown.) As a young missionary he must have been reflecting on terrible events that had happened close by which are described in a book*: 'D asks about 'The Lacquer Lady'; the atmosphere of the book is I think pretty true and the facts about the Palace intrigue and the massacres and the 3rd Burmese War..'* There is a link between a character in the book and someone he actually *knew '....the French lady in the book whose husband was a silk weaver to the Court is alive still: she lives 100 (?) from our compound and though blind is pleased to be visited to talk about the past...'*

He suggests that another character in the book is based on James Colbeck, a missionary in Burma in the 19th century whose *'Letters from Mandalay'*, are a vivid record of many things that happened before and after the 3rd Burmese War. He expresses great admiration for Colbeck, who described how many members of the Burmese royal family took refuge with him, fleeing from fear of death and imprisonment by King Mindon, the father of the last King, King Thibaw .

While writing this letter in Mandalay Christopher must have glanced outside and imagined the gruesome scenes – *'....the corpses would be brought out of the W.gate (the one we usually use being our nearest) and taken down the road past our compound to the Royal Cemeteries just down the road from here; there is a string of bullock carts going now along the route they must have taken...'*

The Royal Palace and moat in Mandalay

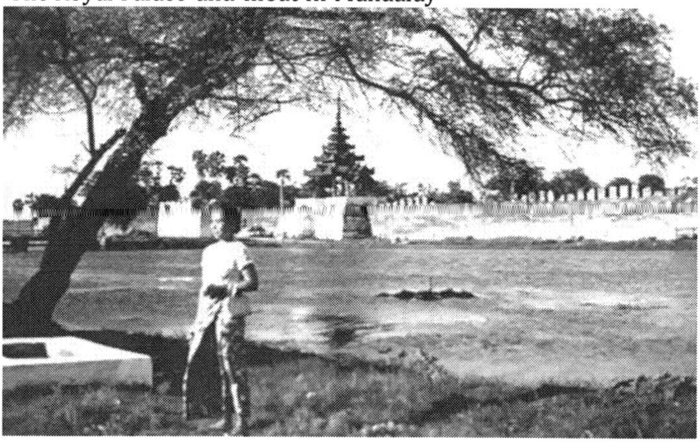

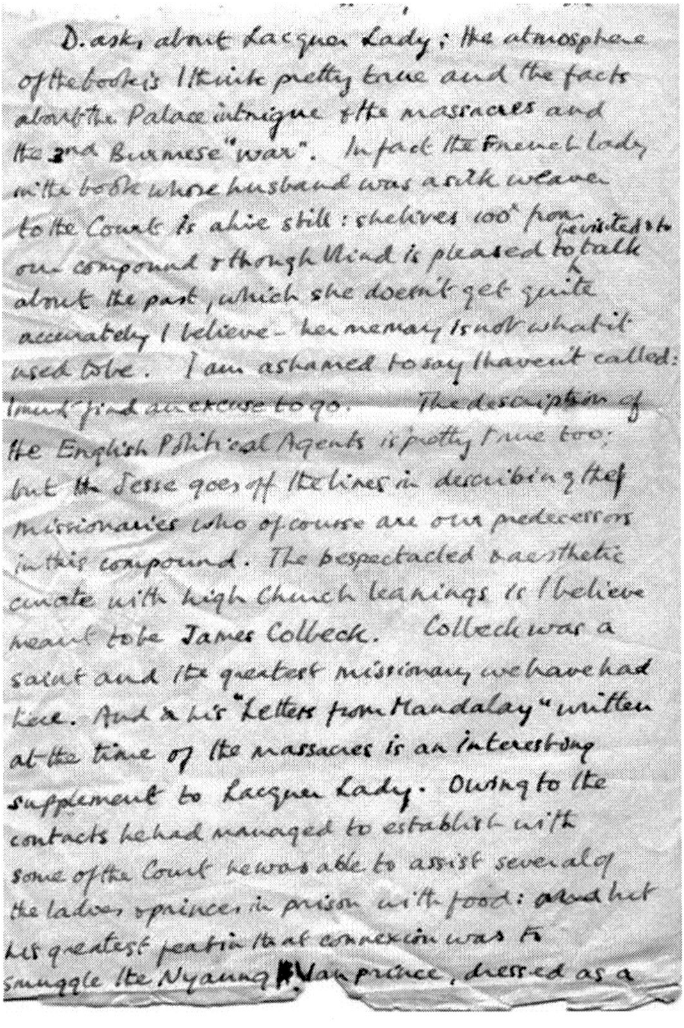
D. asks about Lacquer Lady; the atmosphere of the book is I think pretty true and the facts about the Palace intrigue & the massacres and the 2nd Burmese "war". In fact the French lady in the book whose husband was a silk weaver to the Court is alive still: she lives 100 yds from our compound & though blind is pleased to talk about the past, which she doesn't get quite accurately I believe – her memory is not what it used to be. I am ashamed to say I haven't called: I must find an excuse to go. The description of the English Political Agents is pretty true too; but the Jesse goes off the lines in describing the missionaries who of course are our predecessors in this compound. The bespectacled & aesthetic curate with high Church leanings is I believe meant to be James Colbeck. Colbeck was a saint and the greatest missionary we have had here. And his "Letters from Mandalay" written at the time of the massacres is an interesting supplement to Lacquer Lady. Owing to the contacts he had managed to establish with some of the Court he was able to assist several of the ladies & princes in prison with food: and his greatest feat in that connexion was to smuggle the Nyaung Yan prince, dressed as a

cooly, from this compound to the Political Agent's compound 300ˣ away; where he was safe from attack, and whence he was eventually sent safely down by boat to Rangoon.

I don't know whether Fanny's treacherous revelation of the French Trade agreement is a fact: but quite possibly. She's a historical figure: I believe her second husband is still alive. The French have territorial rights further East in Cochin China next to Siam, and very likely they had designs on Burma.

The Massacres are perhaps overdrawn: but in the main true. The corpses would be brought out of the W. Gate (the one we usually use being our nearest) and taken down the road past our compound to the Royal Cemeteries just down the road from here: there is a string of bullock carts going now along the route they must have taken.

I wish you could read "Letters from Mandalay": We have a precious copy here – but it must be nearly unobtainable in England. Try to get it, though. They are fascinating. His grave is in a little cemetery ½ mile W. of us: I saw it again the other day when I was there trying to find a vacant space for the burial of Daw Shin, ~~when she dies~~, near her husband, when she dies. Daw Shin is the pauper I mentioned who suddenly produced Rupees 200, for this purpose, which she must have kept buried or hidden somewhere in her little house.

In 1878 during the reign of King Mindon James Colbeck described Mandalay as a place of rumours, plots and counter plots. Over a period of time many members of the Royal family and their attendants came seeking sanctuary in his house and he felt he must take them in and hide them. One night Prince Nyoung Yan arrived in a very agitated state dressed as a 'common coolie' and pleaded for help. Colbeck created disguises and got some of them to work in his gardens, arranged escapes and also visited and helped people from the Palace held in prison.

There was confusion about who was heir to the throne. Colbeck heard that apart from Prince Thibau and Prince Mine Tone all others were to be starved to death. When Thibau became King he was dressed in a cloth of gold and a very heavy crown 'like a Papal Tiara' – so heavy he could hardly move. He looked insecure and afraid and did not stay in the public eye for long. With the new King the massacres continued.

It was a time when reports of armed robbery were common with houses being plundered and burned. In 1879 the 3rd Burmese War was not far away, with the British government bringing 5000 additional troops into Burma and sending to India for more. The last King was forced to abdicate by the British and was exiled to the remote location of Ratnagiri in south west India.

In further letters in 1887 Colbeck comments on the fact that there were tens of thousands of Buddhist monks and wonders how Christianity has a chance. However a few months later he writes descriptions of Christian services, and remarks how different things are from 1879. Now the whole of Burma was under the British administration.

The Burmah Oil Company supplied oil. There was increased trade and it became one of the wealthiest countries in South East Asia, with great natural resources of minerals, oil, teak and precious stones. However most power and wealth remained in the hands of British firms, Anglo Burmese and Indians. Armed robbery persisted and many of the local population felt great resentment against the roles played in their society by the foreign power and the many Indians who worked as soldiers, civil servants, construction workers and traders. Officials were appointed to try and stop guerrilla activity in remote regions. When Eric Blair (George Orwell) served in the Imperial Police force in the 1920's there was a 'Burma Allowance' added to his pay to compensate for the added dangers of working there.

The Chinese were encouraged to immigrate to Burma, there was much intermarriage and many were well integrated into life there as merchants, traders and artisans and were active in the House of Representatives. Though there were also some anti-Chinese riots in Rangoon's Chinatown in 1931.

The University of Rangoon was created in 1920 and students began to protest against colonial rule, influenced by Gandhi and Buddhist ideas of non violence. Burmese people who had had the chance to study law in London returned home and worked towards gradual constitutional reform and their increased representation in administrative positions. There were armed rebellions and future national leaders rose to prominence such as Dr Ba Maw and U Saw, Aung San (Aung San Suu Kyi's father) and Ko Nu.

Two Burmese monks U Ottama and U Wizara led nationalist movements, but U Wizara died in prison after a long hunger strike. Uprisings and riots became more violent, and were brutally suppressed by British mounted police and forces made up of different ethnic groups such as Indians, Karens, Chins and Kachins.

'Two racing canoes on Mandalay moat Jan 16 1937 (Viceroy's visit)'

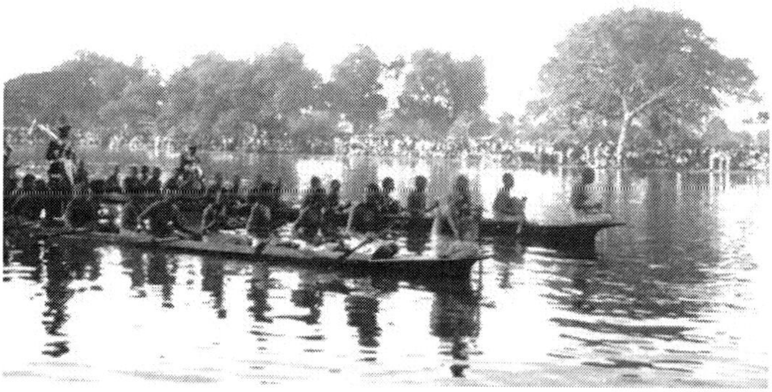

The British separated Burma from India in April 1937. Ba Maw became Burma's first Prime Minister. However there were mixed feelings about this separation, some Burmese thought it was a positive step, but many were still unhappy and riots were common.

In 1941 the Atlantic Charter was drafted and agreed between President Franklin D. Roosevelt and Churchill and supported by many nations, but the wording of the third principle –*'All people had a right to self-determination'*- was open to different interpretations. One American aim was to force Britain to change its policy with regard to its colonies, but in a speech in September 1941 Churchill stated that the Charter was only meant to apply to states under German occupation and not to the British Empire.

Anti-colonial movements were developing in many countries including India and Burma. It is likely that Josephine had witnessed some political troubles as in the diary in February 1942 she referred to the *'school strikes and riots of two years before'.*

Francis Ah Mya, Bishop George West and John Aung Hla

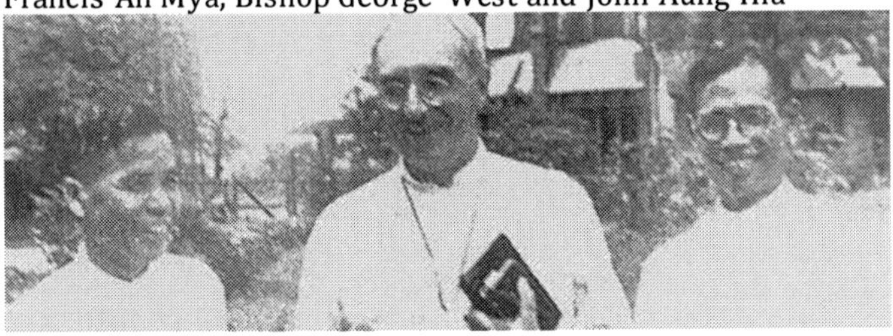

Looking back years later Bishop George West wrote that they were living out the last days of the great British Empire in which Burma was *'a precious jewel'.* Nationalism was rising fast and he recalled how during the war people fled and among them were Miss Ball's little party of orphans from Bishop Strachan's Home, many dropped out from sheer exhaustion and hardly any survived. These were some of the children my mother was trying to help.

She first heard about the war in Burma when a telegram reached her in a remote village on December 9th. During the chaotic days that followed there was still much communication within groups of people she knew, she seemed well informed of events that were going on and mentioned collecting a daily newspaper on Jan 31st. On Feb. 16th she heard of an order for all cars to be out of Rangoon within 24 hours.

There is mention of a visit to the Commissioner's wife in Magwe and a visit to the Club in the evening. There were well organized Evacuations Camps, and sacks of post that were sent from Rangoon to Mandalay. On April 17th there were the resources on the journey to inoculate fifty children against cholera. However transport systems were breaking down under the sheer pressure of numbers of refugees, and shortly after this she wrote *'... no telegraphic communication with the evacuation authorities was now possible.'*

It is approximately 700 miles from Rangoon to Imphal in India – there was a moment when she felt she had to retrace her steps, going back to Mandalay towards the advancing armies and putting herself in danger. Finally she was separated from the others and had to make the decision to trek through harsh jungle country with a group of strangers. She was a master of understatement, and amazingly enough during that eventful and exhausting journey she had moments of exhilaration and dry humour.

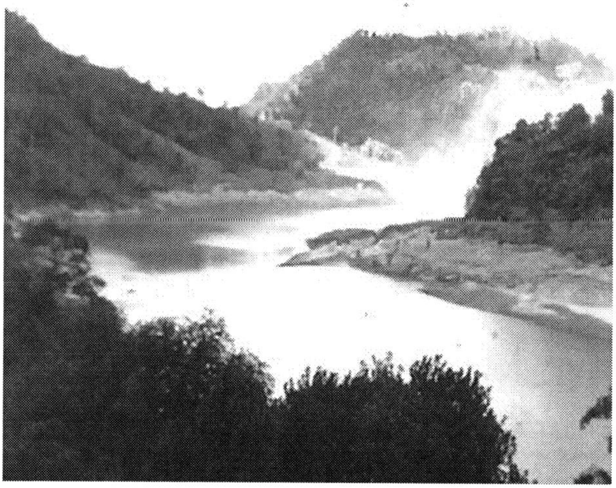

5
Invasion

From Rangoon to Calcutta: The Diary of a Burma Evacuee: Dec.1941 - May 1942

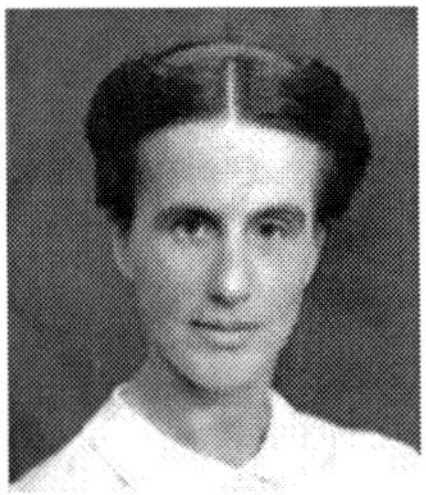

Dec. 3rd 1941 Very reluctantly I set out to catch the river steamer which travelled southward through the night into the Delta. This was my touring season and normally I should be looking forward to visiting the Christian communities in the riverside villages. 'It is alright,' I assured myself as the boat passed the Rangoon docks and turned into the Twante Canal. 'Japan must surely be exhausted after four years in China and would not come this far.' But I wished I were staying in Rangoon. In some ways it is easier to be in the thick of things, and in the jungle I shall get no news at all.'

These are the first words Josephine wrote in her diary. She did not yet know how rapidly the Japanese would invade Burma from the south and the east, and how unexpected and terrifying air raids on Rangoon would throw the population into confusion. She and her companions were about to be forced to travel great distances in 'ramshackle old cars', bullock carts, crowded trains and boats. It is estimated that there were around 500,000 refugees of many ethnic origins, Arakanese, Kachin, Chin and Karen as well as Europeans, Anglo-Burmese and Indians. Many had to make the journey on foot in the intense heat before the monsoon and then subsequently through flooded valleys and jungle. This coincided with the forced retreat of what Allied military forces were then available, their strength and numbers being limited at this time because of huge demands elsewhere in World War 2.

Around this time Churchill summed up the desperate situation in a speech in Parliament. He stated that there had never been a moment when Great Britain or the British Empire could single-handedly fight Germany and Italy, could wage the Battle of Britain, the Battle of the Atlantic, the Battle of the Middle East and at the same time be prepared in Burma and Malaya and the Far East *'...against the the impact of a vast military empire like Japan, with more than seventy mobile divisions, the third Navy in the world, a great Air Force, and the thrust of eighty or ninety millions of hardy, warlike Asiastics.'* He said that if Britain had started to scatter her forces over these immense areas we would have been ruined – '*...We should have cast away the chance, which has now become something more than a chance, of all of us emerging safely from the terrible plight in which we have been plunged....'*

By 1941 Japan held many major Chinese cities, ports and railways. One of its aims in invading Burma was to cut off the spectacular and dangerous Burma Road which was a lifeline for China along which Britain and the U S were sending arms and supplies. This supply route went through Rangoon.

Dec.7th The Japanese attacked the U.S. Pacific Fleet at Pearl Harbour, sinking 4 battleships, destroying 188 aircraft and damaging cruisers and destroyers, with over 2000 Americans killed and 1200 wounded. However at the time three aircraft carriers were absent. The attack caused deep shock to America and led to general support for the U S declaration of war on Japan which followed on Dec. 8th

Dec. 8th Britain declared war on Japan.

Dec. 9th 5 pm I was sitting in the schoolmaster's house in Chaungwa writing a Christmas play for the school children to perform. The schoolmaster was planting beans outside. His wife was bathing her two small children in the river fifteen yards away. I was getting interested in Simeon, having decided that it was he and not the Wise Men who would end my Christmas play. He was going to have a vision of the Cross as he blest the Holy Child in the Temple and off stage the choir was going to sing 'On the third morn he rose again.' That, I thought, would make the message more complete for the non-Christians who would come.
'Mamagyi' said a voice, 'Here is a boy come across the fields from Nyaungngu with a telegram. He says too that the war has begun.' It seemed impossible that the war should disturb the peace of these villages......We rowed from Chaungwa to Shwelaung, a journey of an hour and a half under the stars, so that I could catch the night boat to Rangoon. 'I expect I shall be able to come back soon,' I said.

Dec 12th Rangoon had its first air raid warning.

I was on ambulance duty in the City Hall with ambulance number two. I tried to pretend I was not scared at the thought of taking it out. Nothing happened however.

Dec. 16th Without opposition Japanese forces entered Victoria Point at the southern end of Burma, and they were also advancing from the east through Thailand.

Dec.19th A kindly but firm rebuke from authority. 'Why sit about in Rangoon when your work in the villages is waiting to be done. War or no war the Church has to carry on, and it will go on longer than the war.' I saw the sense of that. One must carry on as normally as possible.

Japan may have been planning to invade India from Burma. The U S hoped Chinese troops would help hold back the advance of Japan in Burma, and Chiang Kai-shek released two armies to fight there.

Dec. 21st I returned to Chaungwa, where we finished off and rehearsed the Christmas play. The schoolmaster had also written one and we rehearsed that too; an interview between the devil and his subordinates when each reported what he had achieved in Germany, Italy, Japan, Burma, England, America, India. They were all very pleased with themselves until the devil asked; 'But what is this I see? Little groups of people in each of these countries saying prayers to the same God? And all the little devils shook their heads and sorrowfully said: 'We cannot possibly stop that however much we try. They are the Christians and today is Christmas Day.' 'You are all useless!' cried the Devil in a fit of rage.

Dec. 23rd We watched aeroplanes flying across. 'Are they British or Japanese?' I was asked. A few minutes later they had killed hundreds of people in the streets and on the docks in Rangoon. The news came through with the river steamer the next day.

Dec. 24th The whole of Chaungwa went off to Nyaungngu for the Christmas gathering of the local villages. That evening each village was to perform its play and on Christmas morning they would all join together in Eucharist followed by a festive breakfast. But I and the Karen lad who always accompanied me, rowed ourselves in Harold Dyer's boat to Gayan where I had promised Shwe Daung that I would spend Christmas Day. That took about four hours.

Rowing along the streams between the long grass and the bamboos, watching the multi-coloured birds and the fleecy white clouds in a blue sky, it was hard to think that the world was at war. As we passed Sabayo a figure in white waved frantically from the bank. It was Evelyn Websper who had come down that morning from Pedaw to assist a Chinese baby into the world. Gayan too was the meeting place for many villages that night. Evensong in the open merged into hilarious merry-making. But they found time to ask me for a talk on the world situation. I wondered what was happening in Rangoon.
Christmas Day A crowded Eucharist was followed by a village breakfast and as we ate our curry and rice, Japanese planes went across. Rangoon had its second air raid.
Dec. 26th We rowed ourselves back to Pedaw where I had breakfast with Evelyn Websper. Iris Miller came over from Nyaungngu where she was staying with her evacuated Normal School from Kemmendine. I returned to Rangoon on the night boat.

Rangoon was a thriving port with a cosmopolitan population including Burmese, Indians, Chinese, Anglo-Indians, Anglo-Burmese, Karens and Europeans. The solid colonial buildings and many wooden houses were all vulnerable in the air raids, and the skyline was dominated by the huge dazzling Shwedagon Pagoda.

Dec. 27th I arrived in Rangoon at 7 a.m. The docks and streets were deserted and there was no transport of any kind. Bazaars and shops were also shut and I discovered later that essential workers from hospitals and post offices had fled. S. Mary's Letter Street and S. John's College had been evacuated because of unexploded bombs in the neighbourhood. I heard how Jean Forrester and Elizabeth Hardy had been on ambulance duty on the 23rd and had both driven ambulances through the streets while bombs were falling and machine gunning was still going on around them I heard too that Alexander, the Divinity student from the Nicobars had been killed at S. John's College. David Paterson turned up from Shwebo. He was to become an army chaplain while the Dyers and Jean Forrester were to go to Shwebo in the north to keep All Saints' going.
Dec. 28th I heard from a lady in the Cathedral congregation how the clergy in S. John's College were enabled to enjoy a good Christmas dinner. She was decorating the church when Padre Moxon said he must go to buy

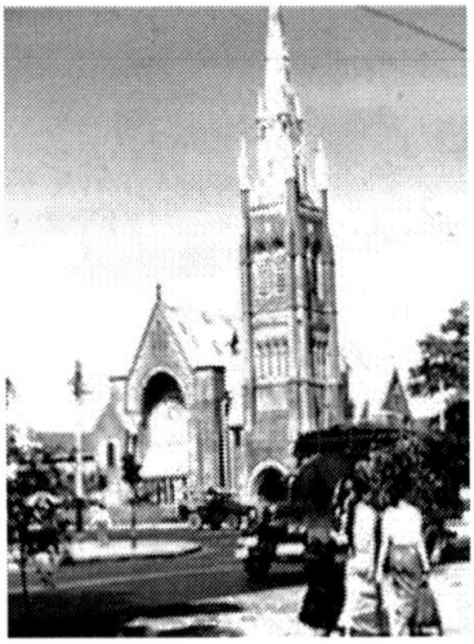

something for their dinner on the morrow. She was not very hopeful as the bazaars were more or less deserted. However, after a few minutes he returned triumphantly carrying two fat ducks. 'I met a man just outside,' said he. 'And I bought them from him They were cheap too.' Later she heard a sad story from a friend who lived two hundred yards from the Cathedral. 'For months,' she said, 'I fattened up two ducks for Christmas, and they were stolen on Christmas Eve.'

January 1942 Jean Forrester went off to Shwebo on New Year's Day, so I felt a little forlorn. I went to stay at Bishopscourt because the schools were all shut. Evacuation of all schools was the main Diocesan occupation at the beginning of January; and a frantic rushing hither and thither became the main occupation of the rest of Burma. Townsfolk fled to the jungle; Rangoon went to the hills and then changed its mind and came back.. Folk from the hills came to Rangoon en route for India, but hearing of a boat sunk in the Bay, returned home again to await further developments.

At this time the Burmese Army was made up of British and Indian units, and there were sixteen obsolete RAF fighter aircraft. There was no co-ordinated military defence of Burma's railways or waterways. On Dec. 12th one squadron of the American Volunteer Group of fighter aircraft (three squadrons had been training to assist China) was moved from Toungoo to Mingaladon near Rangoon.

There was congestion on boats and trains going in every direction, and everybody was fussing around wondering whether Upper Burma or India were better. And meanwhile ugly clouds were gathering on the Siam horizon, thirty miles from Moulmein.

Moulmein was a peaceful colonial town east of Rangoon, twenty-eight miles inland. There were bombing raids here too and many of the population fled to surrounding villages.

The Diocesan Boys' School was taken by Mr. Crouch to Kalaw; the Girls' School by Miss Bromwich and Cecille Allison to Pakokku . Elizabeth Hardy was busy with the hospital which had been opened in her school in Rangoon. S.Mary's Kemmendine was in Nayaunyngu with Iris Miller and Daw Pwa Sein. S.John's College and S. Mary's Letter Street had joined forces with All Saints' Shwebo. The Men's school for the Blind had gone to Kyaukse, and the women from Moulmein to Shwebo. St.Matthew's School from Moulmein had gone to Thandaung; and Bishop's Home was in Kyauktaga, half-way to Toungoo.I went to Prome for a tour of the Chin villages which I had planned with Saya Kya Bu. We had to cut it short as there was no transport .Prome was packed with refugees from Rangoon because it was considered a safe area. But we had an air-raid warning while I was there and rumour was busy.

I returned to Rangoon in the middle of the month to take a party of school children to Miss Bromwich in Pakokku. The train took 36 hours to do a 12 hour journey. That was followed by a 6 hour journey in bullock carts across the sands of Myingyan on the dustiest road I have ever travelled and a five hour journey by river on a a very crowded boat. 'It is all wasted effort to open these up country schools,' said a D.S.P to me on the way. (District Superintendent of Police) *In my ignorance I laughed at his apparent pessimism.*

In a few days I was back in Rangoon. The city was emptying fast and the Japanese were advancing' Moulmein, Martaban, Bilin River, the Sittang. We had moonlight air raids in Rangoon. People were still wondering whether it was sufficient to go to Upper Burma or whether they should go to India. Few of the Mission were now in Rangoon. Irish Miller and Faith Hearn were waiting for a boat to take them to England, Evelyn Websper was still in the Delta. I went off again for another village tour. 'Don't be away too long,' I was told. After all, we still had the KOYLI's (King's Own Yorkshire Light Infantry) between the Japanese and Rangoon. I went to Yeleggi for a few days. 'We are not afraid of the Japanese.' said the Karen Christians. 'It is the Burmese Buddhists who will turn against us when the news is bad.' The local priest confirmed their fears. 'I do not talk to them about it,' Aye Maung confided,' But I know for a fact that many Burmans in the villages are pro Japanese, and we shall not have an easy time.'

There were long standing conflicts between different ethnic groups in Burma which continued after the war. And the attitude of Burmese people to the Japanese invaders was to change.

Jan 29th I returned again to Rangoon. 'I hope I shall be back in the villages soon,' I said. 'We must carry on normally as long as we can.' And as I went along in the ramshackle old car from Yeleggi to Maubin I remembered a conversation I had had some months before with Saya Sein Pu, the Karen padre at Daw-wa. 'The weakness about Christianity in Burma,' he had said, 'Is that we have never had to face trouble. We need a testing.' Little did we know then how soon it was to come.
Jan 30th An SOS from Miss Bromwich at Pakokku....beds, books, crockery are on a sandbank in the river (dry season and water levels low) ...nothing for the children to drink from. I was told to deal with that problem. I went to the telephone. Elizabeth Hardy, Diocesan school......cups, plates if you please for Pakokku.......sorry, they are being used by the hospital I thought again....evacuated YWCA hostel....telephone to track down a member of the YWCA committee ....cups, plates if you please for our school in Pakokku.....I'll consult Mrs. X. Ring again in half-an-hour.
Then an air raid warning and into the trench for fifty minutes. Telephone again ....sorry, Mrs Q has just gone out, ring at tea time. Then at tea time - yes, that's alright. Please send me a list in triplicate of what you borrow and don't take anything not marked YWCA to ensure we get it back.
Jan 31st. Another day to be devoted to cups and plates it seemed. I collected our daily bread from the Savoy and our daily newspaper from the Gazette Office before Service in the Cathedral. Since the bombing we had had to do such jobs for ourselves. Then I went five miles to collect the YWCA Hostel key and returned to Brooking Street in the middle of the town. It was quite deserted. While I was collecting and counting crockery we had an air raid alert. I was tempted to carry on, but I had to remove the car from the open street and was waylaid by an efficient warden who marched me to the shelter in the police station a hundred yards down the road. An hour and a half later we had another warning as I went past the Cathedral with a car full of rattling cups and plates.
In the trench I met Mr Boot, Hugh Wilson and George Tidey, all very cheerful just having finished breakfast. I had not had mine but George gave me half the orange he was eating. We sent the crockery off. Whether it would ever arrive was doubtful A typical day with much busy-ness. But how was one to know what was best to do next?

Feb. 1st I cycled to S. John's for Early Service, but began the day by sitting in the trench with the rest of the congregation: Hugh Wilson and two of his masters who were now in the army, Po Khin and Ba Shein. After an hour we went into church; a few broken windows and some damaged woodwork and much dust.

Feb.5th I went into the Delta again, this time to Nyaungngu to see Daw Pwa Sein, Ma Thit and the remnants of the evacuated S. Mary's Kemmendine. Saya Po Taw in charge of the Nyaungngu Teaching Training course seemed to be the most steadying influence in the village. A Japanese plane dropped pamphlets, showing a caricature of two Burmans tied to a tree and an Englishman in the act of shooting them. Above was written; 'Let us destroy these English who kill our heroes.' - a reference to the school strikes and riots of two years before. But not all the villagers understood the picture. 'Who are these?' I was asked as the questioner pointed to the victims, 'And who is this killing them?'

Feb. 13th I returned to Rangoon. Daw Pwa Sein and Ma Thit came to Shwelaung where I caught the night steamer. The Karen lad and I rowed. I was feeling sorry for him. He had been afraid to tour with me for weeks, but he had done it until now.

There is a long and complicated history associated with the Karen people in Burma who are one of the largest ethnic minorities, and themselves made up of different groups. Some were converted to Christianity and were favoured by the British colonial authorities.

The next day he was going to his own village, and was hoping I was not thinking badly of him. 'Don't tour anymore,' said Daw Pwa Sein, 'It might be dangerous for you, and dangerous too for the Christians with whom you were found. We shall be alright.' Evelyn Websper was still in the Delta looking after the babies.

Feb.14th Somebody who was leaving Rangoon presented the Bishop's Commissary with a cow! It was decided that the children of Bishop's Home now in Kyaukse should have the benefit of the fresh milk, but the Burma Railways had not time to think about transporting cows at this stage, so the creature took up residence in Bishopscourt compound and Iris Miller undertook to milk it. But we waited in vain for a demonstration.

Feb 15th Perhaps Jo did not hear the news that after much savage fighting the Japanese captured the great naval base and fortress of Singapore. This is regarded as one of the greatest British defeats in history. The fast and ruthlessly efficient advance of the Japanese from the north through the jungles of Malaya took the British by surprise, the RAF lost many aeroplanes and the battleship 'Prince of Wales' and battle cruiser 'Repulse' were attacked and sunk off the coast of Malaya. In later years Churchill wrote of his profound shock in hearing this news.

Feb. 16th Rangoon was practically deserted. Hospitals were being evacuated, essential services were more or less at a standstill. The Evacuation Office itself was on the point of moving to Mandalay. Elizabeth Hardy was helping with arrangements to evacuate the hospital set up in her school. George Appleton was on a flying visit to Maymyo. Hugh Wilson was also upcountry for a few days, steadying the diocese. The Sittang Bridge was destroyed.

The Sittang Bridge was destroyed on Feb. 22nd - it was a terrible dilemma because Brigadier Smyth had to decide to blow up the bridge (to delay the advance of the Japanese towards Rangoon) although some of the Indian Army were on the wrong side. The Japanese moved north to find another crossing point.

Pegu would be next and the railway, and Rangoon would be cut off.

The old capital city of Pegu is surrounded by the ruins of a wall and moat and has a rail link and roads going from it in many directions.

In bed that night I remembered the children of Bishop's Home in Kyaukse, halfway to Toungoo. And problems are twice as bad in the night!
Feb. 17th Donald Moxon came to the rescue, and we decided that we must get the train stopped at Kyauktaga while John Matthew and I should go by road to prepare Bishop's Home. But the Evacuation Office had thought before we had. They were going themselves that day and had arranged to collect Bishop's Home as the train passed through, and S. Matthew's school from Thandaung as they passed through Toungoo. It was a relief that everybody we felt responsibility for would be north of Toungoo, and that there were only a few of us left to get out by road.

Hugh Wilson and George Appleton arrived back in Rangoon at midday. We raided Mr Boot's larder to give them a meal.

The necessity to travel all the way to India may not yet have been apparent. Toungoo is a little less than halfway towards Mandalay, travelling northwards from Rangoon. The Battle of Toungoo from March 8th – 25th was prolonged with many casualties, and the Japanese finally took possession of the city after sustained resistance from Chinese forces who had taken over from a small group of British forces.

Feb. 18th The Ash Wednesday Gospel in the Cathedral this morning reminded us not to lay up treasures upon earth. We in Burma quite understood the futility of doing so. Most houses in Rangoon were now unoccupied and much property had been left behind. I should be off myself soon I supposed, and should have to fill the car with tins of petrol and leave my two hundred books behind.

Feb. 20th We saw Iris Miller and Faith Hearn on board a ship sailing for England. There was an order from Government that civilian cars had to be out of Rangoon within twenty-four hours or be destroyed. So we had to go.

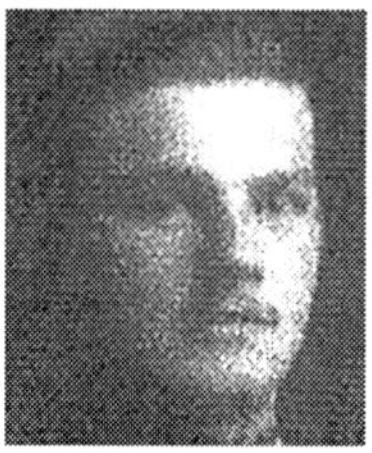

My brother Melrose (Indian Army, at present responsible for supplies and transport in Burma) had arranged to telephone a coded message warning us if the main route to Mandalay through Toungoo was not safe. The message came. We had to go the longer westward way through Prome.

A thousand and one last minute problems. Chief of them was the last minute appearance of three or four Indian servants who a few days before had preferred a sum of money to a free passage to India. Couldn't we take them? And their wives and children and grandparents and aunts and half-brothers and third cousins - about thirty in all? What could we do? There was Canon Harding and his driver and luggage in one car; a Burmese driver and a Cathedral servant in Donald Moxon's car (he himself had joined the troops in Pegu); Hugh Wilson and Evelyn Websper in another car; and I plus a multitude of tins of petrol in the fourth car. Somebody thought of the solution. We could loot the Mission to Seamen's bus which was known to be in their garage. John Matthew would drive it.

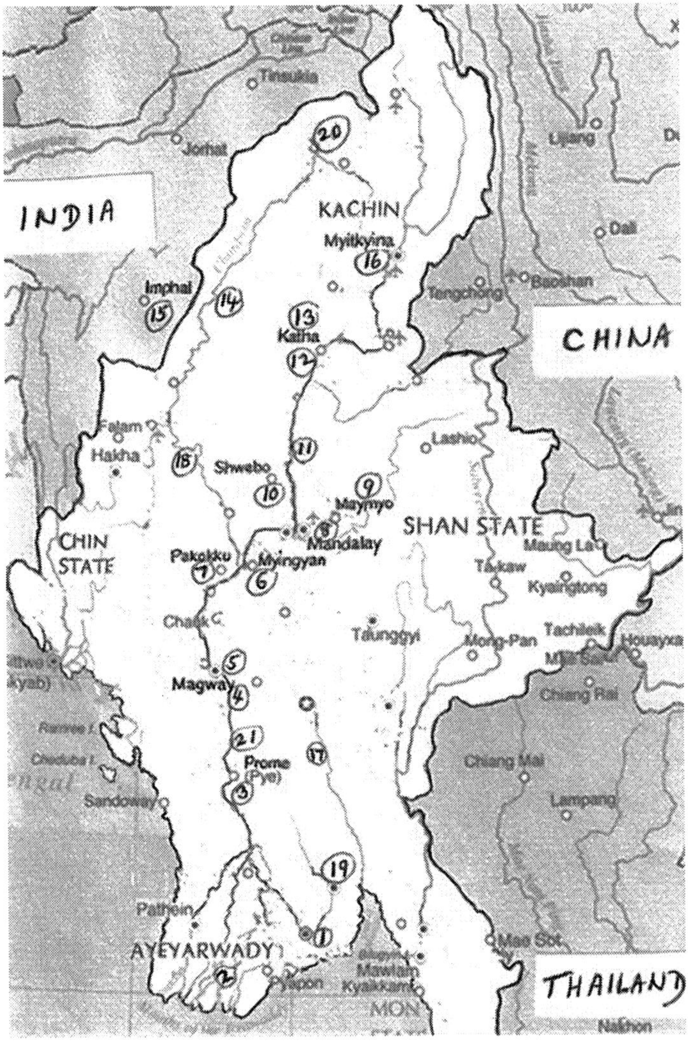

1 Rangoon (Yangon) 2 (Ayeyarwady)Irrawaddy Delta villages such as Shwelaung, Chaungwa and Nyaungngu 3 Prome (Pye) 4 Magwe 5 Yenaungyaung 6 Myingyan 7 Pakokku 8 Mandalay 9 Maymyo 10 Shwebo 11 Mogok 12 Katha 13 Indaw 14 Homalin 15 Imphal in India 16 Myitkyina – strategic airfield taken by the Japanese around May 6th 1942 17 Toungoo 18 Kalewa 19 Pegu (Bago)20 Shinbwigang *'Nov. 2nd All Souls' Day.(1942)...We waited four and a half months hearing rumours and scraps of news now and then. Two thousand people were held up in the Hukawng valley at a place called Shinbwigang, on the other side of a river unfordable in the rains. The track too was knee-deep in mud...'*
21 The great Irrawaddy River which flows south from the Himalayas.

At 4.30 p.m. we left Rangoon. Elizabeth Hardy left the same day with the Dufferin hospital staff. George Appleton left the next day, and the Archdeacon some days after.
Twenty miles out of Rangoon the bus had a puncture. The spare wheel was fixed on with a lock and the key was probably in the Mission to Seamen's garage. Hugh Wilson and John Matthew went back to get it and the rest of us went on to the Irrawaddy.
We arrived after dark and found the P.W.D. full.(Public Works Dept. bungalow) We decided to make it fuller, for driving on strange roads in the black-out was not much fun. The bus and the last car arrived at midnight.
Feb. 21st. Twelve miles from Prome the bus broke down. The cars ahead went on oblivious to the town. John Matthew and a Burmese driver tinkered about while I sat in the driver's seat hopefully trying the self-starter at intervals. Finally they gave up and we had to go into Prome to find a mechanic who eventually got the bus to Prome where it was left in S. Mark's compound. Fortunately it had been arranged to bring the servants and their party as far as the Indian Camp in Prome. Most of us went on to Allanmyo. Hugh Wilson spent the night with Saya Ba Hlet and took the service in S. Mark's on Sunday morning.
Feb. 22nd We went on to Magwe where the Commissioner's wife gave us tea, but we were not allowed to stay. The aerodrome was nearby and Magwe was full. We went on thirty miles to Yenangyaung, and I began to wish we had a spare driver. But it was worth it, for in Yenangyaung we had the parsonage to ourselves. We decided to rest a day and stay there two nights.

Feb.23rd We were able to wash ourselves more than once; find a tablecloth and eat food off plates at a table. We slept most of the day and took a leisurely walk to the Club in the evening to see whom we could see.
Feb. 24th We had Early Service in Yenangyaung Church and set out again. We were now reduced to three cars. The bus had been left in Prome and Canon Harding, impatient with our slow progress had gone on ahead. George Appleton and Elizabeth Hardy also caught us up and went on ahead. We spent the day crossing the dry sandy beds of small rivers, thirteen in all I think. Now and then one car got stuck and we had to push each other out, and once two of the cars had to be unloaded. We passed Myingyan, the dustiest place in Burma, and spent the night in a remote P.W.D. bungalow fifty miles from Mandalay.

It was still the dry season, the monsoon usually started round the end of April and could last from 2-3 months, making travelling much more difficult.

Feb. 25th We arrived in Mandalay. Evelyn Websper and I joined Rosina Simmonds and Dorothy Lewis at the Children's Hospital, and the Winchester Mission House became Diocesan headquarters. One hour after arrival we had an air raid.

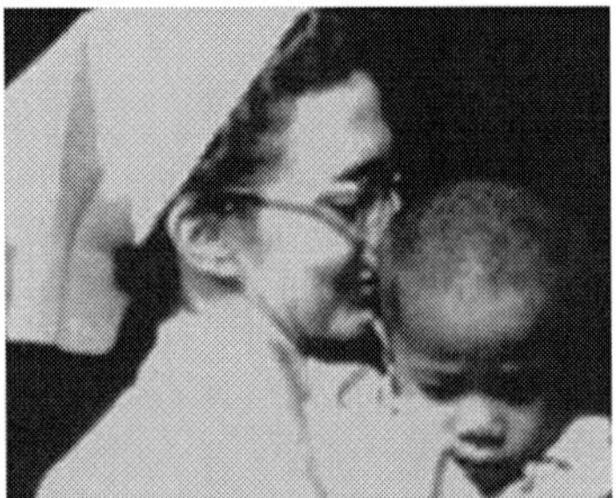

Rosina Simmonds secretly despised trenches as unnecessary for the Winchester Mission. 'I have brought so many Japanese babies into the world in this hospital,' she said, 'I have so many Japanese friends that I am sure they would not bomb this hospital.' However she dutifully sat in the trench every time there was a raid.
Feb. 26th Christopher and Dorothy Lewis sent off by boat to Kalewa on the Chindwin, the first stage on an overland road to India. They were taking care of a woman who had just had a surgical operation and was still on her back on a stretcher.

March 8th The Japanese marched into Rangoon, orders had already been given to evacuate the city and destroy the port and the oil

refineries in Syriam to the south.
(no date given here) *March in Mandalay was like January in Rangoon. The same question was in everybody's mind. 'Shall we go? Is it safe to stay? 'Now there was no longer the sea route. One must either go further north and take a plane to India from one of the few remaining airfields, or in an organized land party up the Chindwin via Kalewa and Tamu.....The Japanese were in Toungoo, but they could not possibly reach Mandalay before the rains broke. In any case the Upper Burma hill stations at least would be safe. Certainly it would be safe in Mogok where the orphans from Bishop's Home and S. Matthew's School had been taken.*

There is hope that airfields in the north were still operating.

Fifteen children came up the river to Mandalay from closed schools not knowing where their parents were. So I spent some days taking them to Maymyo, 42 miles away, to Shwebo 60 miles away, to Sagaing 12 miles away. The advantage of the Maymyo trips was a day of cool weather and the return with a supply of strawberries.

Then the school in Shwebo was closed. Harold Dyer and Jean Forrester were busy with the evacuation camp there, the most comfortable and most efficiently run camp in Burma, everybody said. For me it meant a trip to Mogok to take from Shwebo the children who had no homes; one day on the river and sixty miles up the hill road in a bus. I found people in Mogok were also preparing to leave....ought our orphans to go too? I came back to report. Authorities in Mandalay thought it was unnecessary. It was decided that I should go to Mogok to stay with the school until the war was ended. I was to go after Easter.

This plan was probably made before it was realized how far and fast the Japanese would advance. On April 13th there are efforts to further evacuate the children from Mogok, an area of 500 miles north of Rangoon where rubies and jade are mined.

We spent spare time now and then looking for our letters in the thirty unsorted sacks which had come up from Rangoon; a profitable occupation. One afternoon I found 70 letters for Mission folk and four from my own home.

April 3rd Good Friday. I was sitting in the Mission House with Nelle Linstead. As we talked we heard aeroplanes overhead, either very low or a good number. Were they our own? There had been no alert. Then bombs....very near too, for we were between the Post Office and the Telegraph Office and not far from the railway station.

We lay on the floor on our faces for there was no time to go to a trench. When it seemed to be over, we went across to the hospital to help Rosina Simmonds and her Karen nurses. But Mandalay had begun to burn and the compound seemed to be surrounded by fire. In the afternoon we had orders to evacuate. First the patients; stretchers, lorries and ambulances took them off to other hospitals. We bundled hospital equipment into our own cars and took it down to the Winchester Mission half a mile away. Then our own property from the house, the food, the petrol from the garage and the safe; and then the weary nurses and two little Chinese twins in their cradles, whose parents could not be traced. We drank tea. Returning to the hospital compound for the eight or ninth time that afternoon, I found the clergy trying to extinguish a fire in the chapel roof - no hosepipe, no pump....no ladder....and only water from the well. They saved the chapel somehow.

Padre Garrad returned to the Winchester Mission to find not only his house full, but the school buildings in the compound full too, with Indians, Chinese and Anglo-Burmese people from the bombed quarters of the town. Some wanted rice, some had no salt, and some had no pots to cook in.

And was there going to be enough water in the compound well for everybody? Some had not found a place where they could sleep. And there would be twelve of us for a meal in the mission house that evening instead of three. And where were we all going to sleep? I thought of the feeding of the five thousand. Padre Garrad managed to get there too that night and we ended Good Friday with prayers in Christchurch. We went back to our own house to sleep for the fire had died down in the immediate neighbourhood.

April 4th Mandalay was still burning but in a different part of the town. We brought back from the Mission House what we needed and cleaned up the hospital a little. The clergy cleaned S. Mary's Church for Easter Day. It had been partly damaged by bombing. An evacuee camp was organised ten miles out of the town on the Maymyo road.

Easter Day. I went with Padre Garrad to Sagaing where he took the Easter Eucharist with a congegation of a dozen. Coming out of Mandalay

with its confusion and noise to the peace of Sagaing and its altar made him feel, he said, like the disciples who found their Lord at Emmaeus. I was glad he had come away from it for an hour or two, and I hoped he was taking courage from the Great Failure of Good Friday when he saw the place where he had worked for over thirty years fast being destroyed and his flock scattered hither and thither.
April 6th   Mandalay was still burning in various places. Bazaars and shops were closed and the population was growing smaller and smaller. Chinese troops marched into the town in the late afternoon to take charge of the district. A curfew was enforced on account of looting.
April 8th   Another short sharp raid in the morning. More fires broke out. In the afternoon fires were raging around the Winchester Mission compound, so our cars began running up and down again, this time taking everything the other way. It certainly was a wonderful sight; a wall of fire on three sides of the compound and flames curling round the trees, through the bare branches and over the roofs of the wooden buildings. There was a strong breeze blowing too.

Every time I drove into the compound the fire was nearer...

A frantic effort was made to pull down some of the wooden buildings to save the Church and the Mission House. But the breeze carried the sparks across the treetops and a tree near the mission house was on fire. They managed to beat that out in time. Every time I drove into the compound the fire was nearer. 'Take the church vestments this time' I was told, 'The Church is going to get it in a few minutes.' The next trip I took a sack of rice as well as other things, and broke the springs of the car. The Mission compound was saved while whole areas around were reduced to ashes. The fire died down, and the clergy slept in their own house that night, while the already full compound sheltered more people than before.
April 9th   We had so much property in our house and in the compound outside that Rosina Simmonds and I who were there alone were given a military guard at night. It was a great relief because the nightly fires were getting on our nerves. Now and then we could hear shooting; the Chinese guard dealing with night looters.

Burning debris was flying over into our compound and we had fifty gallons of petrol in the garage.

April 10th 2 a.m. The brewery was on fire and the flames were very high. Burning debris was flying over into our compound and we had fifty gallons of petrol in the garage. I put as much as I dared into the car with the broken spring and asking one of the soldiers to come with me because of the curfew, I took it down to the Winchester Mission. I wondered how many more times the property was to go to and fro between the two compounds. The brewery fire cast a dull red glow all around, queer and uncanny it all felt.
5 p.m. I found Padre Garrad sweeping his compound. He took me to a see a Chinese woman sheltering in the school with her seven children. We thought she had cholera and High Wilson took her off to the hospital. Padre Garrad gave me his last tin of Klim to feed the baby not yet weaned.
April 11th I helped Rosina Simmonds and her nurses to pack necessities. They were going to Mohnyin, the BCMS headquarters and Padre Garrad was to go with them. They would leave Mandalay on the 14th.
April 13th I went to Mogok to arrange for the evacuation of the schoolchildren who were there to India. I was to wait in Mogok until I received a telegram from the evacuation authorities that all arrangements had been made to send the children straight through. By now there was no regular boat service, but I travelled on the steamer which was evacuating the European and Indian staff of the Imperial Bank.

We feared cholera......

We took three days to do a 12-hour journey, during which time an Indian woman died on board. We feared cholera, but were not expert enough to know for certain. I arrived at Thabeitkyin the river port for Mogok at 6 o'clock one evening and was fortunate in finding a bus going up the hill that day. I arrived in Mogok at one in the morning. Miss Lillian Bald and Padre John Derry were relieved that evacuation was being arranged.

Lillian Bald died later during her trek through the mountains.

Jo and her companions had been in Yenangyaung on February 22nd. On April 16th 7000 British soldiers and many civilians were encircled by the Japanese 33rd division at Yenangyaung. Three days later Chinese troops led by General Sun Li-jen attacked and overcame the Japanese –

this was known as the Battle of Yenangyaung. On April 17th the main oilfields at Yenangyaung were destroyed to prevent them falling into Japanese hands.

April 17th We had a few busy days weighing children's luggage, selling school property and stores, holding a jumble sale and getting fifty children inoculated against cholera. I escaped for a walk in the hills once or twice, and the little church nearby was a peaceful refuge in the early mornings. Having just come from Mandalay I found it pleasantly cool too.
I met one of the children loitering on the path way one day searching for something. 'I am looking for rubies,' he explained in all seriousness when I enquired, 'I can take them with me on the aeroplane, they will not be heavy.'
April 21st The expected telegram arrived. Space reserved on the 'Minthamee' on the 22nd. Arriving at Thabeitkyin at 9 am. The D.S.P. arranged the transport for the 60-mile hill road to the river port.

April 22nd 3 a.m. We left Mogok in four buses. The night was dark and there was no moon, and though we were tightly packed with children and luggage, it was chilly and the air was fresh. I wondered which child would be sick first, anticipating that it would be one sitting on the luggage in the middle as far from the door as possible. It was.
The forest fires were a wonderful sight; rings of fire on the wooded hillsides above us and below as we sped down the winding road. This was the time of the year when the jungle folk cleared and prepared fresh land for cultivation in the coming season.
Then came the grey dawn and a chilly breeze; and the sunrise and the day; and the cluster of Burmese houses which was Thabeitkyin and the river. We had ninety minutes to wait on the jetty and then our boat would come...

An agonising wait after an exhausting drive overnight, then fifty tired children are told the boat cannot take them.

....it came at 5 p.m. and drew up alongside, not to take us on board, but to tell us there was no room. The space reserved for us had been taken at the last minute by the hospital authorities in Mandalay and the boat was crowded with stretcher cases.

The children were disappointed and tired too. And we were worried too, for all the boats coming up the river from Mandalay would be crowded, and no telegraphic communication with the evacuation authorities was now possible. We had our evening meal and the children unrolled their bedding on the covered jetty.
We decided what to do. The school party must camp there for a few days while John Derry and I went back to road through the Shan States to Mandalay. A bus was going up to Magok that evening at 7.30. There we could get John's own car from his brother's house and travel all night.

With such pressure on what transport was still available they must have started to feel very concerned indeed for the safety of the children and themselves. Jo's decision to return to Mandalay shocked people who were still there and had thought she and her companions were making progress with their journeys northwards. On this return trip to Mandalay they were very near indeed to danger.

We arrived in Mogok at 11 p.m. and Mrs Derry gave us a meal. But it was windy and wet, and deciding it was folly to attempt a narrow rough hill road in weather such as this, we slept for a few hours.
April 23rd 6 a.m. We set out, John Derry, his brother Dick and I. It was cold here in the hills after the storm. They drove in turn and I slept now and then in the back of the car. The Shan States are beautiful and ideal for a touring holiday. We ate Indian food at dirty little wayside shops and thoroughly appreciated it.
At one point the Japanese were not very far from the road, but fortunately we did not know then and we saw few people and little traffic until we came near Maymyo. I saw the Gokteik gorge and the bridge for the last time. It was destroyed a few days later.

In fact the Gokteik viaduct in the Shan States was not destroyed in the war. Built by the Americans and British in 1900 it was the highest bridge in Burma, the height from the rail deck to the ground is 335 feet and it stretches 2,260 feet from end to end – it was considered a masterpiece of engineering.

We reached Maymyo at 6 pm. The Parsonage was closed and I had a despairing thought that all the mission folk had left. But we found George Appleton and George Tidey in the Military Convalescent Home preparing to go in a day or two. They were very perturbed to see us back. It was too late to go on to Mandalay and we slept in Maymyo. I was really and truly afraid that night, for the school children waiting on the jetty at Thabeitkyin and for myself.

April 24th We went down to Mandalay and arrived just after Japanese raiders had left. What was left of the town was burning still in different parts. I found the Evacuation Officer preparing himself to go north and he was very upset to see me. 'I thought you would all be well on the way to India by now,' he said. 'I reserved space on the boat and in fact went down myself to see it roped off.' We went down to the foreshore three miles away.

In every direction there was nothing to be seen but ashes and debris and burnt out buildings. The Agricultural College was still standing, and the fort with the European houses east of it and the Queen Alexandra's Children's Hospital and the Winchester Mission.

That was Mandalay when I left it. It was deserted too except for the Chinese troops and a few European officials.

The 'Fort' at Mandalay was the Royal Palace surrounded by a moat which had been taken over and renamed Fort Dufferin by the British in 1885 and used to accommodate troops.

We found that another boat was due to leave that evening, a cargo boat being used for evacuees with just one long open deck and no accommodation for passengers. We roped off a place in front, and this time John Derry and I were there to keep other folk out! At 5 pm they were loading fuel when there was a sudden wind storm on the Irrawaddy, a common occurrence at this time of the year. On Mandalay foreshore that meant a sandstorm too.....we should not be able to leave until Saturday morning.

They must have been constantly aware of the impending monsoon, and indeed two days later it poured with rain.

April 25th The boat was crowded with Indians and Anglo-Burmans. Some had no room to lie down .... .wouldn't we let them use our reserved space for the time being? But how should we get them out when our children came on board at Thabeitkyin? I was firm.....so selfish she is ....a Christian missionary too.

'I was surprised to find how nervous I was becoming.....'

I was worried because there were no signs of our leaving. Ten o'clock was the usual time for an air raid and that hour it was not good to be near the railway or the jetty. I was surprised to find how nervous I was becoming. 'God is still around' I said severely to myself. We started at 9 o'clock with a loaded flat attached each side and we went at the rate of two or three miles an hour. I watched people walking along the river bank faster than we were travelling. Twice we stopped to load more wood and we tied up at 6 pm with Mandalay Hill still in sight. When it was dark we could still see too the flames of the Mandalay fires.

April 26th Being well away from European authority, the Indian captain filled my reserved space with Indian evacuees. He wanted the space where they had been to load more wood he said. They would be getting off at the Indian camp below Thabeitkyin. But some of them denied this. I gave it up. God knew all about the situation anyway.

April 27th I sat up where I had been lying down, and while it was still dark and my Indian companions around me still slept, I stepped over their bodies and went downstairs to wash. I had a brilliant idea. I would sit on the roof until the sun was hot. It was clean and there was fresh air and alone-ness, though next time I should bring my blanket for corrugated iron was not very comfortable to sit on. Three hours here in the morning and two in the evening would make the journey more tolerable. I had a number of books too from the Mogok club marked 'not to be taken away.'

That night it poured with rain and the deck was drenched. We crowded even more closely together away from the open sides of the boat.

April 28th We were still far away from Thabeitkyin, but we arrived at the Indian camp at Kyaukmyaung. Some Indians did get off and we managed to clear our space and using what would serve for a broom I swept it in readiness for our children. Japanese planes went across as we were tied up at Kyaukmyaung. We heard the bombs falling in Shwebo, seventeen miles away. We went at a snail's pace.

April 29th We loaded wood again for two hours. Other boats had been passing us and folk began to complain. The Indian captain, it was said, had had orders to return to Mandalay after this trip. He wanted to delay so that there would not be time – and there was not, for the Japanese were in Mandalay very soon after. The captain was making money too from his load of evacuees, charging two annas for a jug of hot water and selling the free rations. The slower our progress, the better for him. 1 pm We reached Thabeitkyin, four and a half days for a twelve hour journey.

'The school party had gone.....'

The school party had gone, but there was a message from Lillian Bald; 'we have waited so long and suppose you cannot get any accommodation. I got a message through to the District Commissioner in Katha and he has sent his own launch down to fetch us. We left at 9 am today. Perhaps you will not be far behind and we shall see you again.' I was now four hours behind them and at the rate we were going, I should be two days behind when we reached Katha. Such a futile effort on my part, but I was glad they had got away and they would certainly be travelling in more comfort.

'The boat did not move at all.....'

April 30th The boat did not move at all. Four Burmese women coolies spent the morning loading nine tons of wood. At noon we were going downstream 200 yards to load nine tons more, we were told. We should not get an inch nearer to Katha that day. Somebody started a campaign for volunteers to load the wood, by making a chain of about fifty people up the bank from the boat to the stack of wood. We passed it down a log at a time. The job was finished in two hours and the captain, very annoyed, went on a few miles.

Jo is feeling exhaustion.

May 1st I lay on my back all day. Carrying sections of tropical tree trunks had not agreed with it.

May 2nd The Japanese took Mandalay.

May 2nd 9 am. We reached Katha. The school party was still there, camping in a wooden house by the railway station, and the town was full of evacuees. There would be no more trains to Myitkyina – the one remaining airfield in operation. Katha was on a branch line, fourteen miles from Naba, the junction with the main railway line. People began walking to Naba, hoping to get a train there. I spent some time in fruitless visits to the Evacuation office and in discussion with authority. Not a hope. I and the older girls must walk out and the younger ones wait at Naba for a mainline train. If no train came, they would have to stay in neighbouring villages.

There were urgent decisions to be made.

The next problem was to find transport for the little ones to Naba, and if possible for the older ones to Indaw, fourteen miles to the south whence we should be in the trek westwards to the Chindwin.
I went to the DSP's house the most likely place to get a meal and the loan of at least two cars. I urgently needed both. I found a dozen Europeans there all preparing to start the trek themselves next day.
The appearance of a young woman at this stage was decidedly a nuisance. They had taken the precaution of sending their own women folk away early, and here at the last minute was another. I understood what they felt, but disliked them for it all the same....they were kind and we had dinner, and I was promised two cars for the next day to ferry the small children to Naba and the older ones to Indaw. I went to bed.
May 3rd 8 am A train had come in! It was a hospital train taking patients from two boats that had just come up the river...no room for civilians. One car took two children to Naba, and the other two older girls to Indaw. On the next trip they would have room for more and we should all be out of Katha by the end of the day.

Jo remains optimistic and hopeful despite the fact that trains are becoming unreliable and overcrowded.

11 am An urgent message from the Evacuation officer. There was space on the train and they could take the school party to Myitkyina...we had them on in an hour. The train was packed. But now there were two children in Naba and two at Indaw. The Naba children could be picked up as the train went through, but Indaw was south of the junction.

Her concern for the various groups of children means that she denies herself a place on the train and becomes separated from her two travelling companions.

It was decided that I should stay and collect them from Indaw, and trek with them if we could not get to Myitkyina. Lillian Bald and John Derry went with the school. I was relieved to get them off. In Myitkyina, even if they had to wait for a plane for a day or two, they would be comparatively safe and not have to trek to India. I was uneasy about the possibility of air raids during the train journey. That afternoon they burnt all the paper money in the Treasury, and having dropped the silver in the middle of the river, they sank all the boats.

In the 1920's the steamers of the Irrawaddy Flotilla Company made up the largest fleet of river boats in the world, carrying some 9 million passengers a year. During the Japanese invasion the Manager of the Irrawaddy Flotilla Company ordered all 600 ships to be sunk, thus denying the Japanese transportation up the rivers.

At 9 pm we had dinner. Mr S who had taken the two older girls to Indaw that morning, told me that he had left them at Naba instead. People were being discouraged from trekking that way for it meant crossing the Chindwin too far south and the Japanese were advancing. It was probable then that the hospital train had picked up all four and I had only myself left to evacuate!

As well as acute anxiety for her own safety Jo had to cope again with confusing accounts of the fate of the children she was trying to help. And there is an awareness of the continuing and fast advance of the Japanese.

May 4th 9 am We had an air raid in Katha. The railway was bombed and evacuees camping under the trees by the station were killed. The house where our children had been camping was burnt down. The European officials left that day, and the SDC took me in his car to Naba. I wanted to make sure that the four children had been picked up by the hospital train. They had. The SDC was going on to Indaw to start the trek to India with his friends. I went with him, though I was undecided about what I ought to do. He left me at the PWD bungalow at Indaw where Major D gave me tea and said I must start the trek in his party. But I felt I must try to follow the school party to Myitkyina to make sure they were safely on their way and to help Lillian and John. 'Very well,' said Major D, 'a military train will be going through in an hour or so. I'll tell the station master to find you a seat on it.' I sat on the station for four hours, but there was no train. At 8 pm Major D came back. 'Come and have dinner,' he said. 'There will be no train after all.'

Jo has a disappointing four hour wait for a train which never came. Did she feel very alone at this point? She begins to realize that she will have to start walking to India……

I should have to start walking to India tomorrow. There was a conference in the PWD bungalow. We had a meal on the grass outside and spreading out our bedding there, lay down to sleep. It was cool and the stars were bright.

Bishopscourt, Rangoon

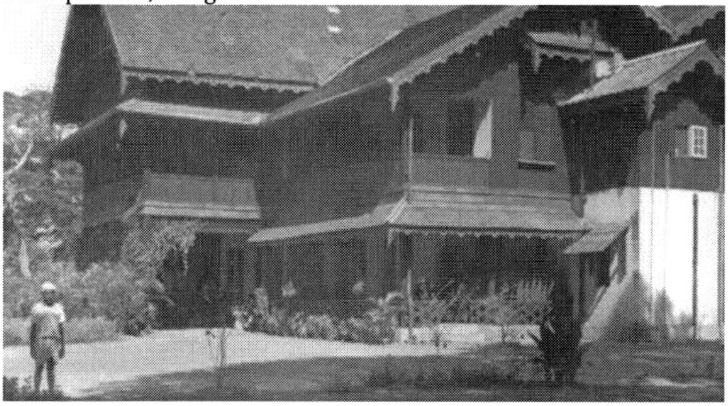

Karens

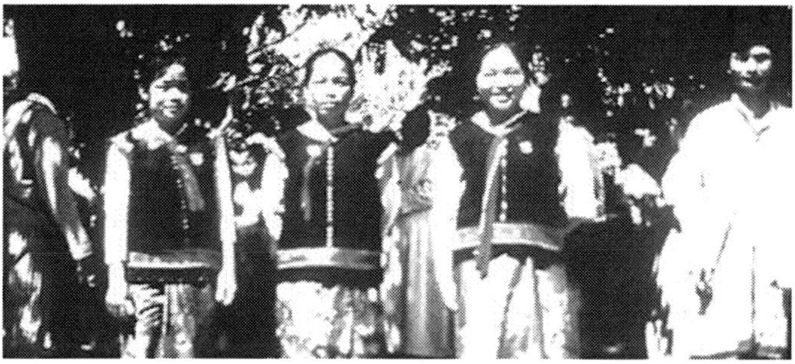

'Celebrating Holy Communion in an air raid'

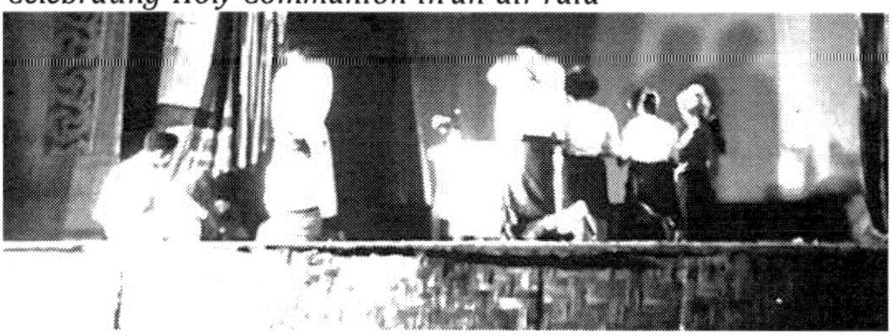

Pegu

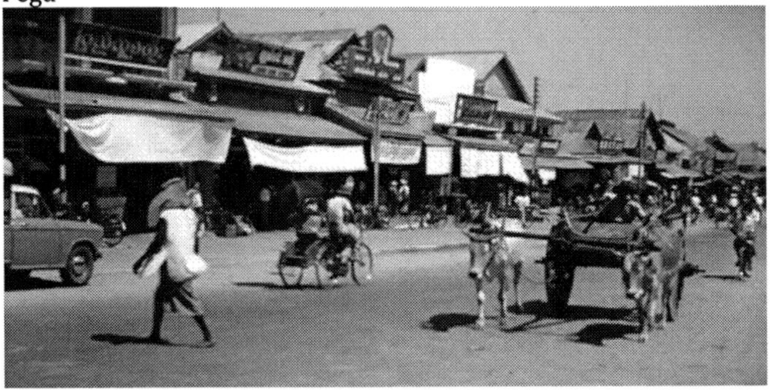

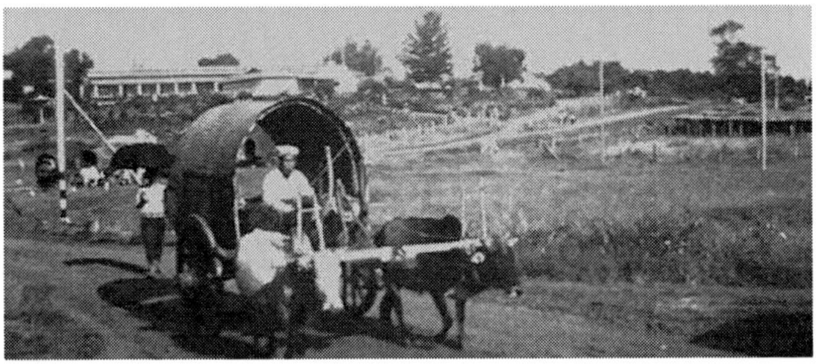

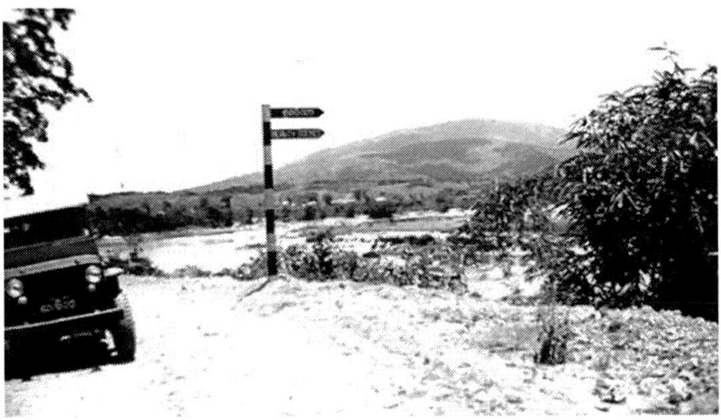

Mandalay

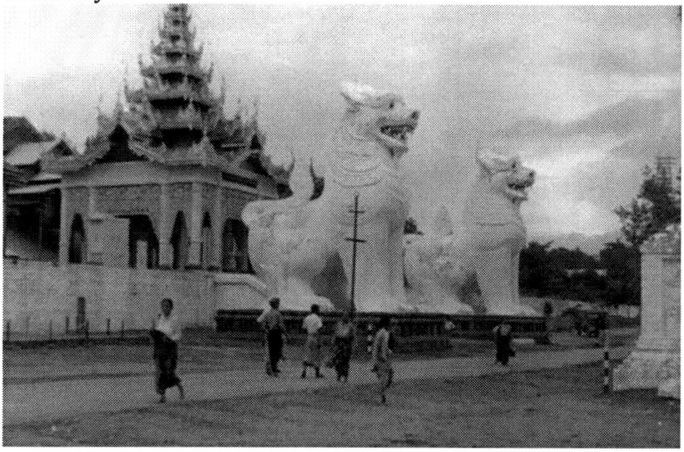

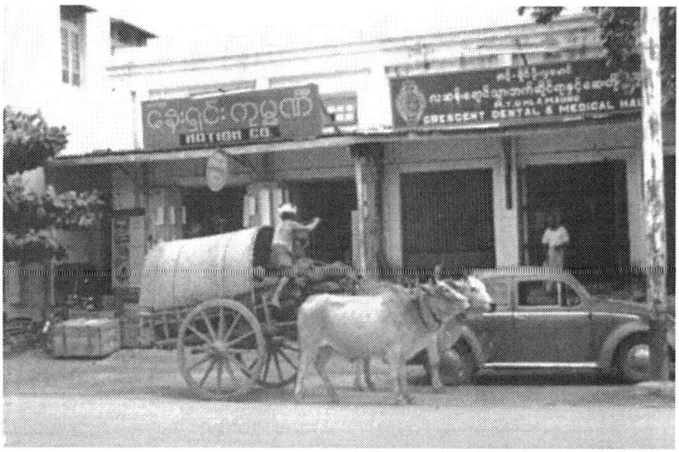

One of the compounds described in the bombing raids

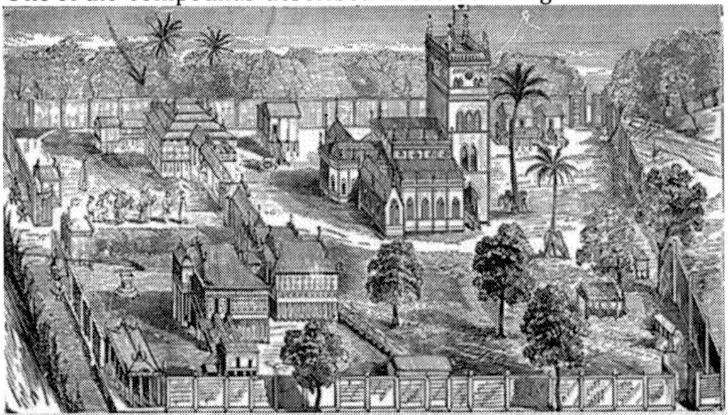

THE MANDALAY MISSION COMPOUND, CHURCH, SCHOOL AND CLERGY HOUSE
(An old wood-cut from the painting by a Burmese artist).

Maymyo market

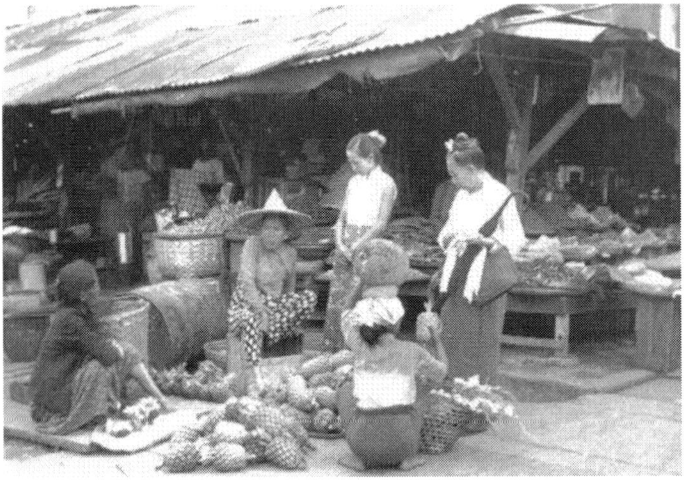

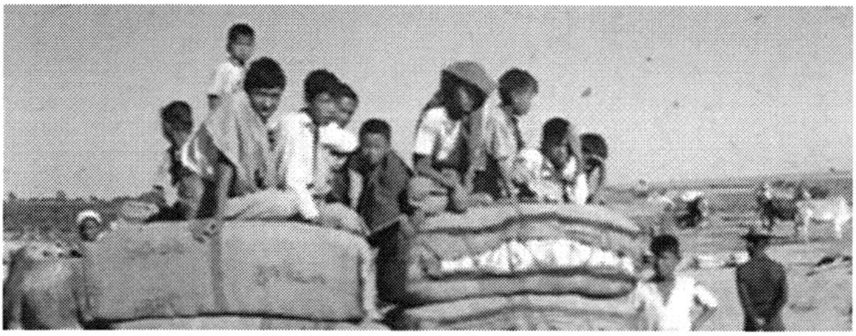

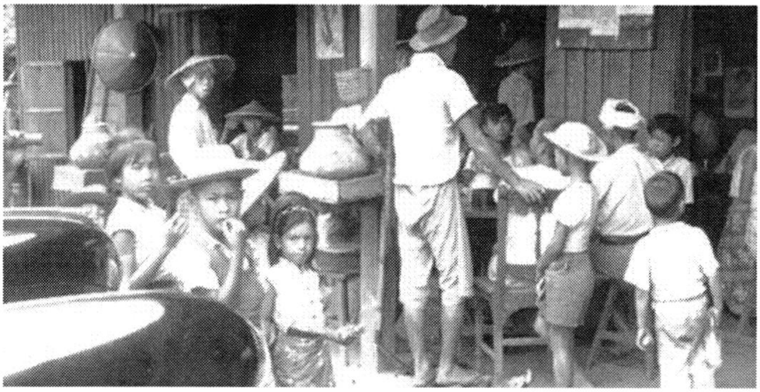

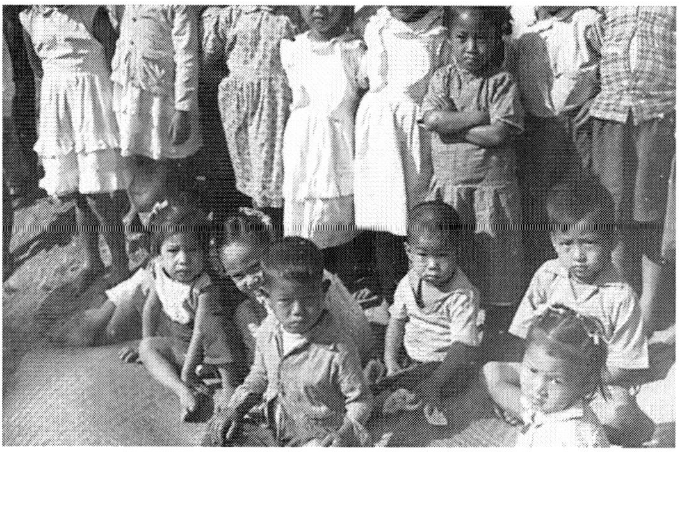

View from a boat of *'the distant pagodas at Sagaing'*

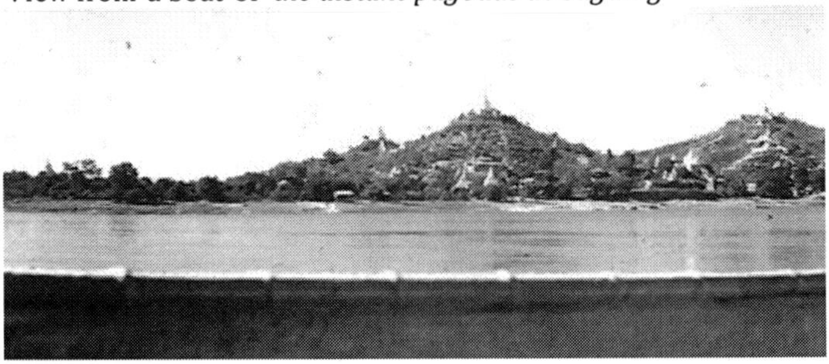

Scene by a river

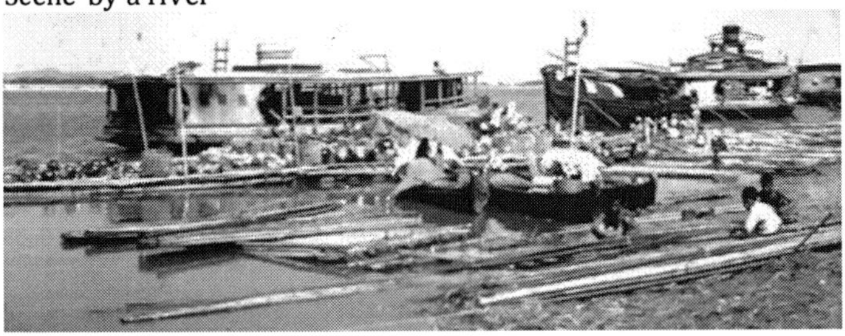

Looking down on a ruby mine

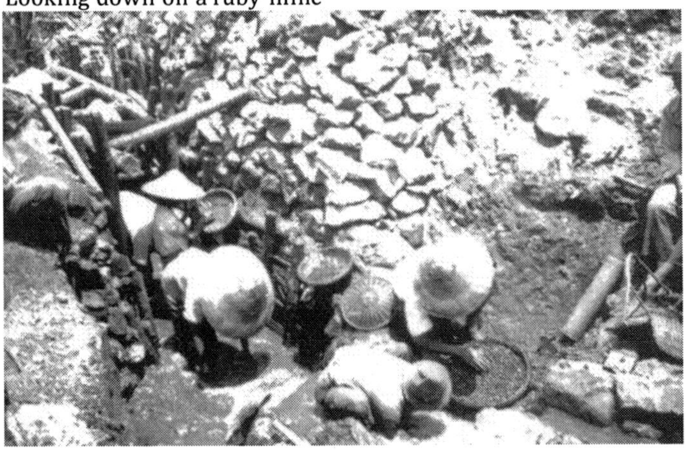

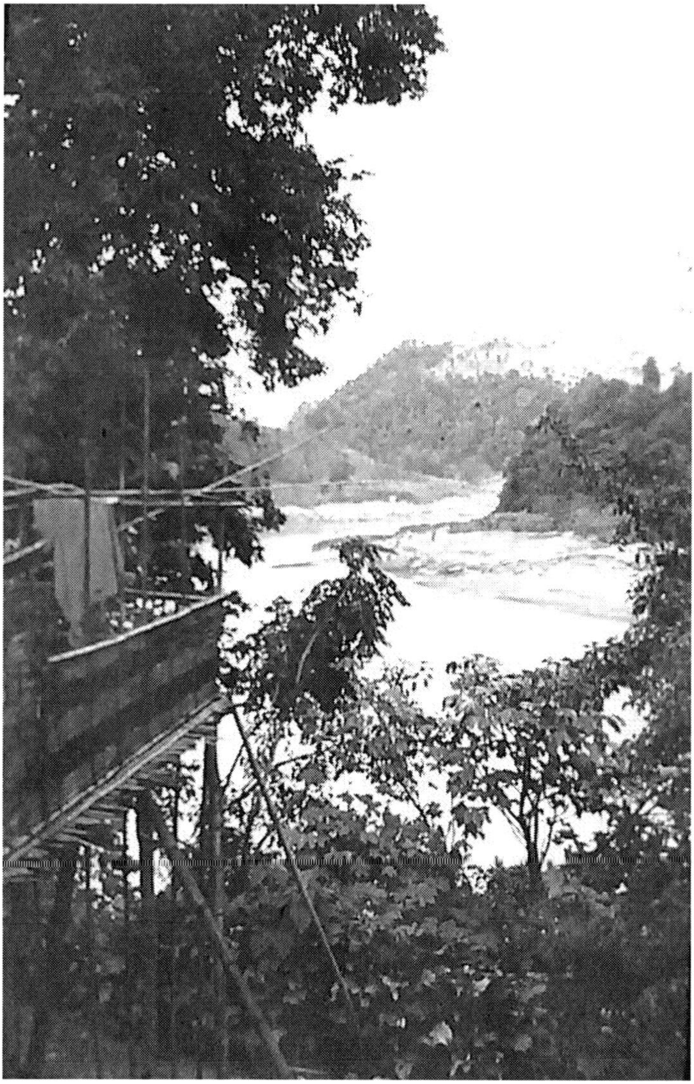

6
Walks through the jungle

'I.... was determined that the party should not be held up because there was a woman in it...' Josephine

May 5th I was up at dawn. I sorted out what remained of my property. I had to carry it myself. I reduced it from 25 pounds to 15 pounds by leaving among other things, my Bible and prayer book and diary. I hoped my memory would be reliable.

This is puzzling - what became of the diary?

I had to carry my rice rations. At the last minute Major D could not come, and I was sent on with three Burma business men from Rangoon. We were taken the first forty-six miles to Pyinbone by car, and having slept in the heat of the day, we walked fourteen miles by night, arriving at Mansi with the dawn.

May 6th We walked all day too, about 15 miles. I could not see any sense in getting so tired, but was determined that the party should not be held up because there was a woman in it. We were trying to overtake another party I was told. My luggage was heavy and I threw my blanket away. 'You will need that in the hills,' I was warned. But I could not see the sense of carrying it in the heat for three weeks for the sake of three or four cold nights. We passed the body of a soldier face downwards in the grass with his kit around him....we did not overtake the other party and slept in the jungle near a village called Magyigone.
May 7th We found the Evacuation officer and his staff, about 40 in all, at Kyauksegyi at midday. They were camping on a good site near the U-Yu river.

I was thankful to find six women in that party, and thankful too to rest. We stayed there two nights, for as we were to follow the course of the river for two days, it seemed wise to spare ourselves as much as possible by travelling down on rafts, and they had to be built. Somebody gave me another blanket and quinine tablets with strict orders to take them every day because I had no mosquito net.

May 9th There was trouble with the villagers about the rafts which they had undertaken to build for us. They would not be ready for another two or three days. Even when they were, progress down the river would be slower than walking. We divided the party and those who wanted to walk left at four that afternoon. We had a few Indian servants who carried our kit, and a horse to carry the rice.

Finding the track through the hilly and thickly wooded jungle very difficult, and impossible in places for the horse, we decided to wade through the river. Being the end of the hot season, the river was low, and in the deepest places reached only to one's thigh. Fortunately the river bed was sandy and one could comfortably walk barefoot and spare one's shoes.

All Sunday and half Monday we walked in the river. It was tiring but cool. We slept in the open at night. On Sunday afternoon one of the Indian servants was bitten by a snake. An Indian doctor in the party made an incision around the bite and we waited to see what would happen. But only a swelling, and the man limped for several days.

There would have been snakes, leeches, flies, ticks and mosquitoes, and diseases such as malaria, dysentery, cholera and typhus.

May 11th We left the stream after our midday meal, cutting across fifteen miles of hilly country to join it again at a place called Mainkaing. On Monday night we had a violent storm as we slept in the open. So putting on our raincoats, we sat on our bundles to keep them dry. At 3.30 a.m. the servants lit a large fire. How they could do it with such speed when everything is drenched after rain, I shall never understand. We dried and warmed ourselves and drank plain tea.
May 12th 11.30 am We reached the river again at Mainkaing and had breakfast in the PWD bungalow. Then we bathed in the river and sat in various states of disarray while we washed our shirts and shorts and dried them in the midday sun. Here we were able to get a raft and we set out at 4 pm. Such enjoyable anticipation: a day or two gliding lazily down the U-Yu river to the Chindwin...after a few minutes we stuck on a sandbank, and we all got off to push the raft clear. We spent the rest of the day going about half a mile having to cope with sandbanks all the time. We tied up at dusk by a sandy clearing, ate the last tin of beef with

our rice and went to bed. There was another storm that night - and another fire in the early hours to get dry and warm.
May 13th The raft was cut into three with the hope that each section, being lighter, would avoid the sandbanks. But it was not much better and we travelled about only five miles. We should not get to Homalin in a week at this rate. And meanwhile, where were the Japanese? We had been warned that we should cross the Chindwin by the 15th.
May 14th We abandoned the rafts at midday. We walked hard that afternoon and found a PWD bungalow in which to sleep that night. It was fortunate for we had another storm. The sole of my shoe was coming off and I tied it on with a bootlace.
May 15th We walked early and hard and reached the Chindwin at 9 am . Burma is very beautiful; the crystal clear river; the deep green jungle beyond; the purple-blue hills outlined clearly after the rain against the morning sky; the lights and shade of their curves and valleys. We followed the river for several miles before stopping for breakfast and our midday rest.
We were told not to go the Homalin but to cross the river some miles to the south. At 4 pm we were able to get country boats, hollowed-out tree trunks which could take five people. We all reached Tonhe on the other side at 7.30 pm after dark.. The village was crowded with evacuees, but - our fortune seemed too good to be true - the school house was standing empty.

Somebody went in to investigate, and found the bodies of two cholera victims. A storm was threatening so we managed to crowd into the already crowded houses. It does not need much space for a bedding roll on the floor. Somebody managed to buy a tin of milk no doubt looted by the seller from stores left here and there for evacuees. So we had a choice on the menu that evening: milk in the tea and plain rice, or milk on the rice and plain tea. We had dessert too, for the householder sold us a kind of sugar candy made from the toddy palm.

May 16th We began the hard walk over the hills into India. It was a relief to be across the Chindwin because we were now going away from the Japanese instead of towards them. But we were still racing against time for the monsoon would break soon. Each day our programme was the same. At 5.30 we got up and drank plain tea, filled our bottles with boiled water and set out. We walked until 11.30 resting for five minutes each hour. At midday we ate our breakfast of boiled rice and then rested until 4. We walked again until 6 o'clock, had our evening meal of boiled rice and went to bed. On the first day the trek was rough and in hilly country, though there were no difficult climbs.

May 17th Today we had a sheer climb for about three miles up a rocky mountainside. The cool breeze on the top was delicious and the view was grand, though clouds partly hid it.

There were hospitable villagers in this district where we found houses for our midday meal and for shelter at night. Unfortunately they sheltered other living creatures too and it was not always possible to sleep. The nights were cold too.

Our sack of rice was stolen, but a village headman sold us some more, and allowed us to shoot a small pig. We lived on pork for a day or two.

May 18th The rains broke, but we walked doggedly on. At midday we reached a village where we hoped to have breakfast and dry our clothes, but some British soldiers there told us to move on as quickly as we could. 'We have a case of cholera in this hut.' We spent a bitterly cold night in a draughty house at the height of 4000 feet.

May 19th We met some more military folk in a village. One of them had just died of cholera through drinking river water two days before....I had done that twice since I left Katha when I was hot and had had no boiled water left in my bottle.

…….trekking out of the war into it…….

My shoes could stand no more, and I left them on the wayside. An Irrawaddy Flotilla Company captain gave me his spare pair, size 8 - a little large. We heard that Imphal had been bombed either once or twice.... trekking out of the war into it. The jungle had its trials, but at least it was free from bombs and machine guns.

As we ate our evening meal of boiled rice and tea, we indulged the animal man by discussing what we should eat first when we got to Calcutta. I chose chocolate and cheese, a pound of each to begin with would do.

May 20 We set out in the pouring rain. Raincoats were wrapped round our kit to keep blankets dry, and I had left all warm clothes behind when I thought I was going by plane. We went 17 miles this day because it was cool. The first eight were in the hills where we were exposed to wind and rain.

But it was grand country and never before have I been among such lively, fast-moving clouds, now filling the valleys, now hiding the hills. How the wind blew! I hurried because I was so cold.....'Stop this wind and this rain, I can't bear it and I am freezing right through' - I offered the Almighty a very childish prayer. And then I laughed to think that I should expect God to change the course of the monsoon because one insignificant mortal was chilly in the hills. 'All the same,' I went on, 'You could give me some warmth from inside myself, couldn't You?'

'...the highway to India, two feet wide and six inches deep in mud....'

At a fork in the path a notice on a tree pointed to the right. 'To India' it said. The highway to India, two feet wide and six inches deep in mud. We took the road to India, a steep winding descent of three miles into the valley.
The path was now more like a rushing stream. We reached the village at midday and found tinned provisions for evacuees and a hospitable villager who lent us his house; one large room with a blazing fire in the middle of the floor. We got warm and dry.
In the late afternoon we went on for a few miles. We were now in Manipur State and at dusk we reached a village of high caste Hindus. We had to pay heavily for permission to sleep on the verandah of the village granary. But it was the cleanest village I have ever seen in the East; as neat and trim and as well laid out as an English suburban housing estate.

May 21st. A few miles from the Manipuri village we reached a road and Yaripuk where we had a good meal in the PWD bungalow. We went by lorry to Imphal. It was more or less deserted except for the military.

At this time the town of Imphal was built up to be a base for the Allies with airfields, camps and stores of supplies and held by part of the British 14th Army under Lieutenant General William Slim.

We heard news for the first time for nearly three weeks. The Japanese were in Myitkyina on the 6th having come unexpectedly, not up the railway or the Irrawaddy, but overland from the east....the schoolgirls with John and Lillian had come to Myitkyina on the hospital train on the 3rd. They would not have arrived before the 4th....2 days to get away.

She feels more anxiety wondering what has happened to the children at Myitkyina with John and Lillian. It is not until much later that she hears news. Myitkiyina airfield was of great strategic importance, and during the time it was occupied by the Japanese the Allies were forced to make dangerous flights between India and China, known as ' flying over the Hump'.

May 22nd It rained hard all day. We went 133 miles by lorry from Imphal to Manipur Road railway station, a narrow winding road crossing the hills at nearly 6000 feet. We arrived a 8 pm and had dinner in the Teaplanters' camp. So civilised and clean and comfortable.
May 23rd At 5 am we started the long journey on the train to Calcutta.
May 25th Whit Monday 7.30 am. I went to Bishop's House and ate eggs and bacon with the Bishop's chaplain, Padre Tucker and with Canon Caldicott who was also from Burma----the luxury of a hot bath.... And some home letters....but the school party had not arrived from Myitkyina.

There follow some fragmented accounts of what happened to others on their journeys to safety. They are included here just as they appeared in the diary, not necessarily in chronological order.

Nov. 2nd All Souls' Day. We waited four and a half months hearing rumours and scraps of news now and then. Two thousand people were held up in the Hukawng valley at a place called Shinbwigang, on the other side of a river unfordable in the rains. The track too was knee-deep in mud. The RAF was keeping them supplied with food and after the rains they would come through, we were told. Our children were probably in that camp.

Thousands of refugees were forced to try and make their way to India through the treacherous Hukawng Valley and steep mountainous forests. The Japanese 33rd Division halted on the Chindwin at the end of May.

So we waited and on October 15 we received definite information. The smaller children were being sheltered at Sumprabum in Upper Burma, and although they were safe, they could not be brought through until after the war. But then a telegram came; twenty three small children had arrived in Assam. I was sent to Gauhati to meet them, and found them in a better physical condition than any evacuees I had seen. Some had had malaria and were not very fit, many had sores, but they were lively and very talkative. They were surprised to see me. 'Somebody told us you were dead,' was the cheery greeting of one child. I responded, for they did not seem to have grasped the real tragedy of it all;

'I walked all the way,' I said 'and raced you even though you came on an aeroplane.' We brought them to Calcutta. Eventually they went to a well organised Burma evacuee camp in Bangalore in S.India.

The hospital train from Katha reached Myitkyina on the evening of May 4th, and with hundreds of other evacuees, our party waited on the airfield for a plane. On the 6th they were still there and were scattered by an air raid. Later in the day a plane was brought for the, 'Bishop's Home children' - they were called.

But they were some distance away and some of them were very small. When they arrived the plane had gone. It would have been folly for the pilot to wait long. In any case he would have soon had as many passengers as he could take.

But the Japanese were almost there and all the refugees had to be ordered out of the town. They went in military lorries or on foot. Our party was taken to the hundred and second mile where the way divides.

From there the older girls and boys with Lillian Bald and John Derry and a few other adults began the trek along the Hukawng valley. Two military men accompanied them.

The smaller children, thirty in all, were taken by lorry to Sumprabum thirty miles in the other direction. They stayed in the PWD bungalow in Sumprabum, and the military, before they left, gave them 70 bags of rice. An Irish Roman Catholic priest, Fr. Stuart, who was there was given money also to help them. For a month they lived in comparative comfort, but on the 15th June Chinese troops arrived and took all the food they could find. Mrs D who with her own four children was there also, managed to hide a few sacks. But she took fright and decided to trek to India with her children and two or three other adults.

Fr. Stuart took the other children to a village two miles away and cared for them there for three months. They were in the care of one of Fr. Stuart's Jinghpaw Christians and were comparatively well fed all the time. But Fr. Stuart himself had other work to do in Ki's large district and often he was away. Three of the children died in those three months.

Twelve-year old Eileen, being the senior of the party by three years, seems to have mothered them all. 'We were a long way from the stream,' she told me, 'and it was cold. So we did not bathe much, and we had no clothes to change so they were not washed at all.'

In July the Japanese came, but they did not interfere. In fact they gave the children food now and then, and Eileen had a blanket and pullover that a Japanese soldier gave her.

'We were singing hymns one day,' she told me. 'And the Japanese soldier came along to listen. He knew English a little and said he was not a Christian but had been in a Mission school and knew those hymns.' Another day they heard him singing: 'Jesus loves me, this I know, For the Bible tells me so.' On September 10 two British officers arrived from Putao, eighty miles away. They promised food which was dropped by plane five days later. On October 5 they brought elephants and took them all away. They arrived in Putao on the 13th where they bathed and were given clean clothes! From there they were taken by plane to Assam.

There were thirty-six in the party which began the trek with the two soldiers. There was little food and on some days they had practically none. On the way were many other refugees in the same plight: malaria, dysentery, cholera, exposure, exhaustion. And they slept in the jungle at night in the pouring rain. The day came when they could go no longer and they stayed in a village while the two soldiers went on to get help. One died on the way and the other arrived exhausted, but before help could be sent back, an Indian soldier from Burma arrived in the camp. He had passed through that village at the end of August, he said ....It was too long a journey for school girls in the Hukawng valley in the rainy season. God in his mercy had ended it.

The diary ends here and is signed
J B Chapman

By May 1942 Burma was in Japanese hands.

After Rangoon was taken the Allied forces tried to hold the north of the country with the help of Chinese troops. However the Japanese divisions had been joined by soldiers from Singapore and the Allies were forced to make the decision to retreat. Due to communication problems almost none of the Chinese troops knew what was happening, and some travelled to India where they were put under the command of the American Lieutenant-General Joseph Stilwell who spoke Chinese. But there were others who fled towards China through hostile countryside where many perished.

There are other accounts of escapes from Burma. In the following article we read of the ease with which the Japanese forces invaded Burma from the south, together with tributes to the courage of the Allied forces and memories of the devastation of war.

EXTRACTS FROM ARTICLE 'THE BURMA POLICE AND THE RETREAT FROM RANGOON' by J R Manning, (2)

I served with the Burma Police in Rangoon before the war......When Singapore fell to the Japanese, we knew it would not be long before we would be their next target, so a lot of us enlisted with the newly formed First Burma Division, and after six weeks training, some of us were posted to Moutmein in Southern Burma, under General Wavell. In 1942 the Japanese landed at Victoria Point, the very southern point of Burma - there was nothing to stop them, nothing at all. Our first serious fighting against the Japs took place at Moulmein.....The Military Forces in Burma, when the shooting started, were hopelessly inadequate. The two good British Battalions, the 1st Bn Glosters 28th Foot, and the 2nd Bn KOYLI suffered heavy casualties, and the only formation in the field was the 1st Burma Division. We were poor in quality, less than half-trained, ill-equipped, and in no condition to face the Japs. Overall the Japs were generally well equipped........ what I feel was outstanding and magnificent was the spirit and courage of the 14th Army, who, against all odds, fought tooth and nail against these inhuman savages - I feel very proud and that to me is the real Burma Star spirit. When Toungoo, Prome and Pegu fell to the Japs, it seemed to us that the fate of Burma was sealed......We were told to make our way to India, and keep our weapons against treacherous Burmese and Jap snipers, many of whom seemed to lurk in almost every tree, while every hilltop sheltered a gun, plus attacks from the air.

I have never ever seen so many people of different nationalities lying dead by the roadside, and hundreds of others fleeing in fear of their lives, -it was absolute chaos. I believe it was a journey of 700 or 800 miles or more, I'm not sure. The sun will never set on the memory of the gallant men and women who fought and died, no matter what rank or what job was done. Faces, places - the names are beyond recall... In conclusion I would like to say, graves known and graves unknown will always be remembered, and never forgotten - gone from our eyes but not our hearts.

And in the following extract from an article written by Dr. E Eason there is detail about the dangers of walking through the 'dense and trackless' jungle and the fear he experienced when he was left temporarily in charge - the leader of the group went off to investigate the sound of shooting nearby and there was a possibility that he may not have returned. Some people mentioned here were still able to get a plane from the airfield at Myitkyina.

There are parallels with Josephine's account, the destroying of personal possessions, the use of boats and bullock carts, the sense of danger near the Chindwin river, mention of the U-Yu river and Homalin, the shooting of a pig, the routine of walking and surviving from day to day, the thirst and hunger and ever present threat of disease. Something Jo does not mention is the leeches which could attach themselves to the body when walking through the rivers and streams.

EXTRACTS FROM 'BURMA 1942 RETREAT'
A Doctor's Retreat from Burma' by Dr.E Eason (3)

'........ I went to India and thence to Burma just before Pearl Harbour as a C.D.O. in an Indian Field Ambulance. After a short stint at the front in Lower Burma early in 1942 I was invalided to the base at Maymyo owing to deafness and put in charge of No.2 Burma Field Laboratory as I was good at microscope work — diagnosing malaria, dysentery, V.D., etc. where deafness was less of a handicap. When the enemy swept northwards I took to the field with my unit which was attached to a C.C.S. When the order came to run for it we were somewhere on the railway north of Mandalay. We trained up to Mogaung and our patients — unfit people, those over 40 and women (nurses,etc.) went on to the rail-head at Myitkyina and were flown back to India. The rest of us walked. Our party

was in the charge of a British I.M.S. major who was an old Burma hand, knew the country and the Chin language ...... Before starting our walk from Mogaung we destroyed anything that might have been useful to the enemy. I threw my microscope, etc., into a nearby lake but retained the "oil-immersion lens", an especially expensive but small article which I gave to one of the B.O.R.'s.

..... From Mogaung to Klwegyi, about seventy miles, was easy going through country inhabited by the Chins, and for part of the way we were able to hire bullock-carts. It must have taken about five days. We had plenty of rice and bought chickens, eggs, limes, melons, etc. from the villagers..... The chief problem was water as streams and springs were not very frequent,......

I had a brief bath in a slow flowing river (or canal) and came out festooned with leeches. The chaps gathered round them by touching their tails with lighted cigarettes which made them let go — we still had cigarettes at this early stage. Klwegyi was on a tributary of the Uyu Chaung and here we managed to get sampans for the next leg of the journey. Down stream to the confluence with the Uyu about two miles north of Schedwin and thence down to where the Uyu joins the Chindwin at Homalin was about eighty miles, but easy going apart from a bit of rowing at which we took turns......

.... A few miles short of Homalin we heard shooting. This might have been the enemy who were advancing northwards, so we parked on the river bank and the Major and one other went on by themselves to investigate, telling me (the senior officer left) that if they were not back in an hour I was to lead the party back to India as best I could. I realised that this would have been virtually impossible with no map, only a compass, through dense and trackless jungle and not knowing when I was likely to hit on a track or meet the enemy. It was pretty unnerving to say the least as I would, almost inevitably, have been responsible for the deaths of all my men as well as myself. However, I assumed a nonchalant air and to my im-mense relief the Maior returned inside an hour. ..... So we all re-embarked, went on to Homalin and started the eighty-odd-mile trip to Imphal in Manipur State (India).

This was the worst part because, although the path was easy to follow it went across mountains and very steep ravines. As we had to carry our rice, water and a few essentials everything not essential and weighing more than a few ounces had to be jettisoned, and I threw away a pair of spurs which I had since my Yeomanry days and which must now be at the bottom of the Chindwin. We did about ten miles a day to keep pace with the slowest, starting before dawn, and each evening the Major asked all the men whether they could do the same again and they all could (just). By this time we felt fairly safe from the enemy but there was a temptation among the younger and fitter to hurry on ahead to get back to the safety of India quickly. One of the advance guards did just that and I believe was court-marshalled for desertion. There were quite a few civilians, mostly Indian women, escaping from the Japs along part of our route all in poor condition with children. This was the most harrowing aspect of the whole thing as our job was to get ourselves back and not to get bogged down with civilians. In a moment of weakness I gave one of them a drink from my water-bottle which I ought not to have done. Some were dying of cholera and/or typhoid which none of the soldiery got because they had been vacinated...... A colourful incident occurred when we camped by a Naga village. The Nagas were much less civilised than the Chins, and their practice was to shoot one of their pigs when wanted for the pot. We bought a pig and one of our B.O.R.'s who was armed with a rifle, shot it, ... Although thirst was worse than hunger on the first leg of our walk, they were both equally bad on the last leg..... The success of our escape was largely due to the Major (Raymond) who was a good leader and organiser. On the whole we were a happy crowd with a minimum of jealousy and disagreement, but we were lucky to get across the Chindwin in time to escape the enemy and lucky that the monsoon was just over which made travelling easier......'

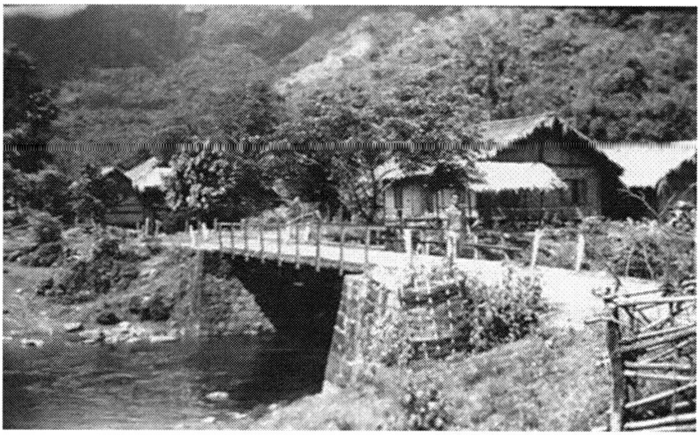

'....country boats, hollowed-out tree trunks which could take five people.'

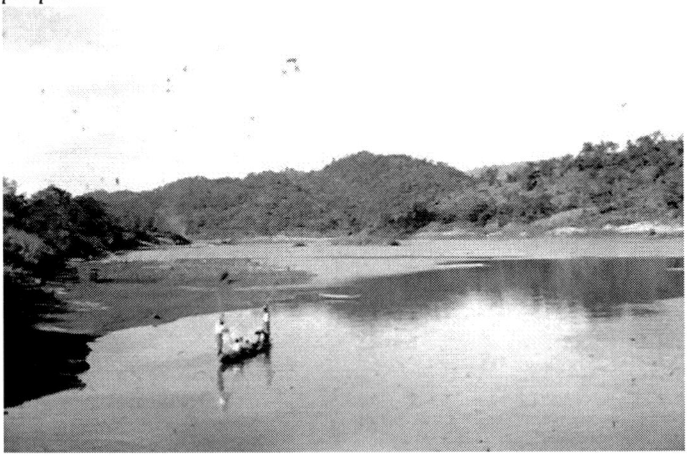

'Later in the day a plane was brought for the, 'Bishop's Home children' - they were called. But they were some distance away and some of them were very small. When they arrived the plane had gone. It would have been folly for the pilot to wait long. In any case he would have soon had as many passengers as he could take....' (p 85)

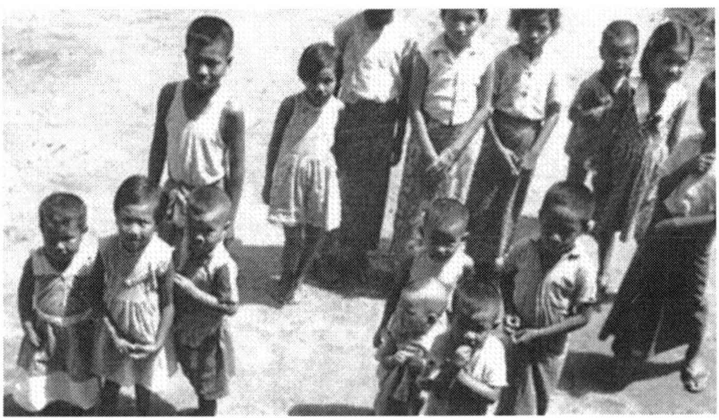

7

The Burma Campaign and a veteran's account 1942 - 1945

'...The Way was to begin at Chittagong and then go through the Arakan to Paletwa on the Kaladan River, a distance of approximately one hundred and ten miles. It had to be carved out of dense mixed jungle, mainly bamboo, and it proved to be a mammoth task, mostly done with pick and spade...' John M Ellis 2012

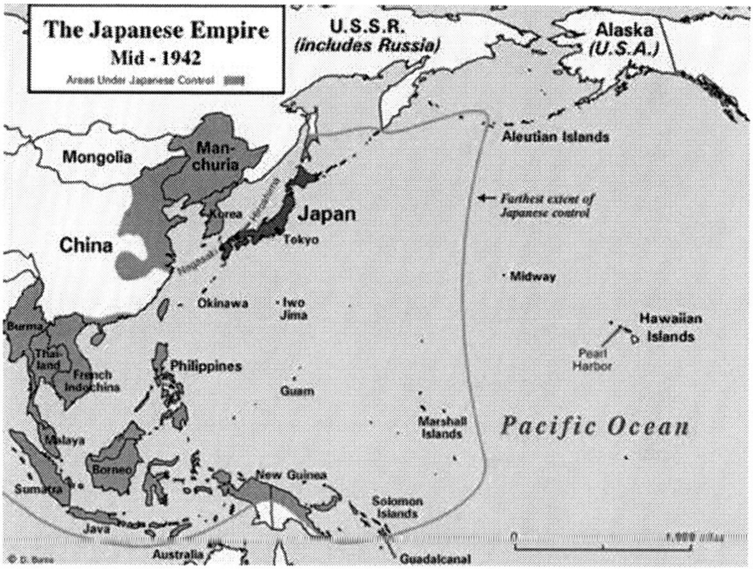

At the height of its power in 1942 the Japanese Empire dominated a land area of approximately 2.8 million square miles. Emperor Hirohito, the 124th Emperor reigned from 1926 – 1989 and many Japanese regarded him as a god - *Arahitogami* is the concept of a god who is a human being. The Emperors were considered to be descended from the goddess of the sun and the universe, *Amaterasu.*

Hakko Ichiu was a Japanese political slogan that was revived to reinforce nationalism. It is a saying with ancient origins, interpreted as meaning that imperial rule had been divinely ordained to expand until it united the entire world. In the 1930's Emperor Hirohito was associated with this slogan and the expansion of military power was justified in terms of bringing people together under the emperor's fatherly benevolence, thus giving reasons for force against those who resisted. The 'Way of the Emperor' was considered a moral way and inspired extreme loyalty.

Hakko Ichiu was contained within a white paper published in Japan in 1940 which proclaimed that the aim of Japan's national policy was: *"the establishment of world peace in conformity with the very spirit in which our nation was founded"* which led to aims to establish the Greater East Asia Co-Prosperity Sphere.

George Appleton (later Archbishop of Jerusalem) wrote an account of a meeting at Nyaung-ngu the day before the evacuation of Rangoon was ordered. .... he told the village people that he was willing to stay if it would help. Their reply was that the presence of a missionary might cause them to be in more danger. He remembered sad and loving farewells said that evening and being taken out in a sampan to board the last river steamer to go to Rangoon. '*...Many of us were never to meet on earth again.*'

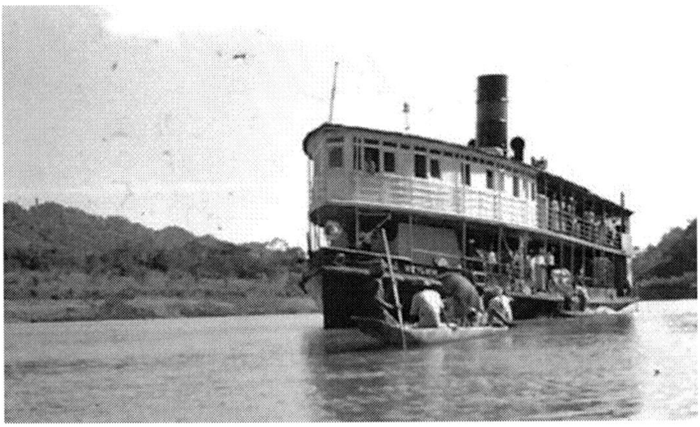

Bishop Francis Ah Mya of Rangoon wrote about his experiences in the war years. After about a year of the occupation he ventured out from where he had been living in the hills and came to Toungoo, about 65 miles by foot, by train to Martaban, by launch to Shwegun and to Kappali where he was heading. He said the situation was so bad and insecure that he had to leave the very next morning. The journey to Kappali and back took nearly a month, sleeping at railway platforms and river banks, and running for safety at the approach of bombers and fighters. *'Malnutrition, disease and deaths were common every day scenes'.*

From June 1942 Japanese troops had reached northern Burma and many Asian civilians and prisoners of war were used as forced labour to build the Burma railway and what became known as the Bridge over the River Kwai through mountainous jungle. Huge numbers lost their lives, some reports suggest as many as 90,000 local civilians from Burma, Singapore, Malaya, Java and Thailand, and thousands of Allied prisoners, British, Indian, Australian, African, and Dutch, some of whom had been brought to Burma from prison camps in Singapore. Many died from sheer exhaustion, intense heat, malnutrition and illnesses such as cholera, dysentery and malaria.

The Burma Campaign was fought by the forces of the Commonwealth, China and the U S, with many land forces drawn from India and Africa, and it was complicated by the monsoon rains, the difficult terrain and communication problems. From 1942 there were failed attempts by the Allies to retake Burma. Many Chinese soldiers were capured by forces from Thailand who controlled some eastern areas. In July 1943 Lieutenant-General Renya Mutaguchi was appointed to command the Japanese army in Burma. He wanted to invade India and cut the Allies' lines of communication in northern Burma where attempts were being made to build the Ledo Road to link India and China by land

In August 1943 the Japanese proclaimed Burma to be an 'Independent Nation', but many Burmese who had initially hoped for an end of domination by the British came to realise this was a much worse situation. Meanwhile the Allies were short of resources because so much war effort was being concentrated elsewhere in Europe and the Middle East. And violent 'Quit India' protests happened around this time in Bengal and Bihar requiring the use of British troops.

There were two Allied operations during the dry season 1942-3, but

Japanese tenacity and their ability to travel in the tough terrain proved too difficult to overcome at this stage. Colonel Orde Wingate's Chindit expeditions started developing new tactics – Chindit was a name they took from the stone tigers that guarded temples in Burma. They marched deep into Burma damaging communications of the Japanese but suffering high casualties. However their successes improved morale and helped the British and Indian forces believe they could fight and survive in the jungle. The progress of the war in Burma was soon going to change.

In October 1943 Churchill appointed Lord Louis Mountbatten Supreme Allied Commander of South East Asia and he obtained more air support for the 14th Army. He personally travelled great distances to make himself known to companies who were widely scattered in dangerous locations, and inspired the troops with his dynamic leadership. In one of his speeches to the troops, he is reported to have joked with them that though they thought of themselves as - '*The Forgotten Army on the Forgotten Front...*' in fact nobody had even heard of them, but all that was going to change. He was going to supply them from the air, and people would be hearing about their victories...'

The Japanese often camouflaged themselves where they had dug themselves in. Allied soldiers were encouraged to rely on air dropped supplies and hang on to their positions. They would attack when the Japanese least expected it, using the jungle for cover and keeping in contact by radio. The Gurkhas took part in the Burma Campaign and are famous for their bravery, strength and resourcefulness in the jungle, having been recruited from Nepal where qualities of great physical stamina had been developed during childhoods in the harsh countryside. And Merrill's Marauders were a US Army special operations unit who were admired for their deep penetration missions behind Japanese lines.

The Japanese got as far as Imphal and Kohima in India near the Burmese border. The Battle of Imphal lasted from March till July 1944 and the Japanese were driven back into Burma, and began to suffer from falling numbers, lack of supplies and illness caused by the harsh conditions and climate. The morale of the Allies had improved under Lord Mountbatten's command - this was a turning point.

The Battle of Kohima was fought from April to June 1944. It started before the monsoon and Lord Mountbatten spoke to the troops; he said that the Japanese would not expect them to fight on during the monsoon, but that they would, and whatever they needed to support them he would supply, mainly by air. British and Indian reinforcements strengthened the troops to drive the Japanese from their positions on the Kohima-Imphal road. So it was at this point that the Japanese plan to invade India was brought to an end.

During the Battle of Kohima the British and Indian forces lost over 4000 men and the Japanese over 5000, with others lost through starvation and disease. Here is an extract from Admiral Lord Louis Mountbatten's Address to the Press, August 1944:

'My object in this Press conference is to try to put before the Press of the world that every effort has been and is continuing to be put into the South East Asia campaign; ......'The South East Asia Command is a long way off: it is apt to be overshadowed in Europe by the climax of the war against Germany and in the Pacific by the advances of Admiral Nimitz and General MacArthur. Therefore a major effort by Allied forces, doing their duty in inhospitable places, has been some-what crowded out and the forces have not received their propor-tion of credit. My purpose this afternoon is to put their achieve-ments before you. .....

"Enemy-held territory in the South East Asia theatre extends 2,500 miles southwards from the north of Burma. The front on which we are at present fighting in Burma alone extends some 700 miles and is second only in length to the Russian Front. It is the hard land crust which protects the Japanese conquests in China and Indo-China. It is Japan's land route to India and, more important, the Allies land route to China. Both offensively and defensively Japan has strained and is straining every nerve to hold Burma. ....

"Before 1943 there were no roads into Burma from the north; while the lower reaches of the Brahma-putra river are unbridgeable. Assam is, in fact a logistical nightmare. Moreover, advancing as we are from the west, we are fighting against the grain of the country, for its steep jungle-clad mountains and swift flowing rivers, all running north-south, constitute a barrier instead of a route between India and China. ......

"Even more deadly and persistent in inflicting casualties is the mosquito. Malaria has conquered em-pires and can cripple armies. In the British campaign in the Arakan in 1943 it inflicted a particularly heavy toll. The zeal and skill of American and British medical services have succeeded this year in reducing the ravages of malaria by no less than 40 per cent;

particularly effective has been the development of advance treatment centres which have virtually perfected a lightning cure. More than 90 per cent of the patients report fit for duty after three weeks. All the same, since the beginning of the year Allied forces have suffered close on a quarter of a million casualties in Burma from sickness, mostly malaria and dysentery...'

In late 1944 there were plans to launch offensives into Burma, from the sea into Arakan on the west coast, from the north on the newly constructed Ledo Road and from Imphal across the Chindwin into central Burma where the terrain became less inhospitable. The Chinese National Revolutionary Army continued an offensive from Yunnan province together with American assistance.

To some extent reinforcements of infantry, lorries, pack animals and equipment were prevented from reaching the Japanese army in Burma. The Indian National Army - initially made up of Indian prisoners of war from Singapore who had been given the option of fighting alongside Japan – began to feel alienated by being denied equipment and supplies and being used as labourers.

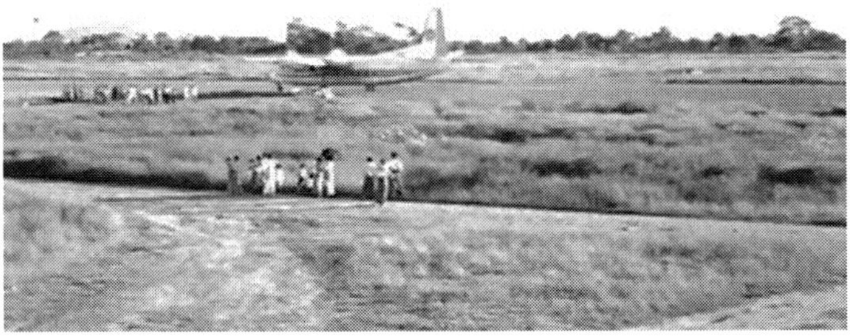

The important port and airfield at Akyab Island in the west was eventually retaken by the Allies at the end of 1944. Progress was made securing the western coastal areas, and airbases could be built to supply troops inland.

In 2012 John Ellis recalled his part in the Burma Campaign, looking back 69 years. He describes the advance down the west coast, and the backbreaking task of cutting the way through dense mixed jungle by hand with picks and spades.

John Ellis Photo taken in West Africa

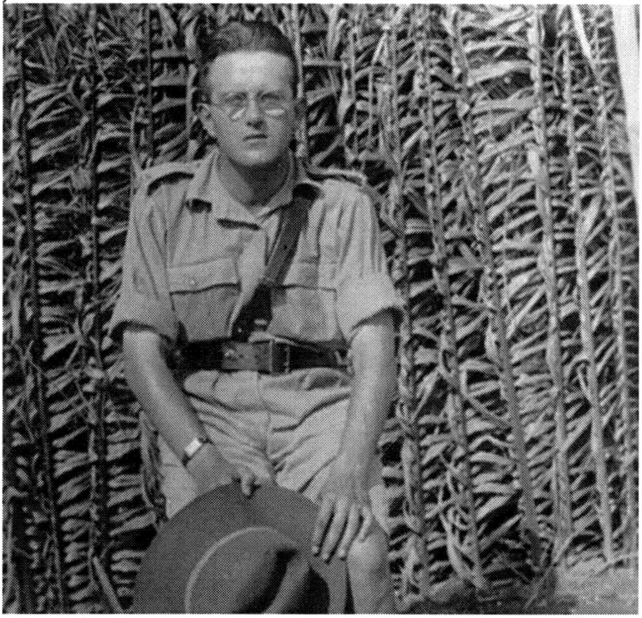

'I served firstly with the 4th Auxiliary Group, Sierra Leone Regiment, then with the 1st Battalion of the Gambia Regiment, both being in the 6th Brigade, 81 Division, the Royal West African Frontier Force, and later, after recovering from wounds, with the 3rd Battalion The Gold Coast Regiment, 82 Division, The Royal West African Frontier Force. In June 1943 we sailed from Lagos, Nigeria to India, and disembarked at Bombay.

In late 1943 we went into Burma. I was wounded on 7th April 1944 in an ambush near Misawa, a village on the east bank of the Kaladon River, by a burst from a Japanese machine gun.

1st Gambia's activities were in the Arakan, and in the Kaladan valley, with the objective of capturing Akyab in conjunction with the other units comprising 81 Division.

The initial task of 81 Division was to make what was to be known as West Africa Way, so that vehicles could bring supplies, ammunition and equipment to support the advance down the Kaladan to capture the port of Akyab from the Japanese.

The Way was to begin at Chittagong and then go through the Arakan to Paletwa on the Kaladan River, a distance of approximately one hundred and ten miles. It had to be carved out of dense mixed jungle, mainly bamboo, and it proved to be a mammoth task, mostly done with pick and spade.

Whilst working on the Way in Bengal, no Japanese interference occurred, but thereafter in the Arakan fighting was frequent.

The tasks of reconnaissance to locate the positions of Japanese forces and to gain knowledge of their probable moves were often carried out V. Force. This consisted of patrols of about ten men each, commanded by a British Major, and composed of personnel from Indian Intelligence Units, and others well acquainted with Burma and the Japanese. One of the tasks of V. Force was to spread alarm and despondency among the Japanese. One example was that our Africans were in fact cannibals, and that terrified them.

The Japanese were usually small men, and many wore spectacles. However, some were tall, such as the Imperial Guard which attacked one of our positions in the Kaladan Valley, led by a Colonel Tanahashi. When Japanese positions were taken, life-size rubber women were sometimes found – comfort for their troops.

Often, when we were to cross a river to deal with the Japanese on the other side, they could not be seen in the thick jungle, and launching our assault boats and then getting in them, and then waiting for shooting as we crossed the river, was quite disturbing, but often the Japanese had melted away, leaving no opposition.

Burma, I found to be, was a beautiful country, and I well remember the white mist like cotton wool over the rivers in the early morning; the abundant wild life, such as a flock of yellow budgerigars in a tree of red blossom.

When fighting was over, and we were in Rangoon prior to taking our Africans back to Africa to demobilize them I bought two watercolour pictures by a Burmese artist – one was of Fort Dufferin at Mandalay, and the other was of a female dancer (a Karen, I think) at the Court of Thibaw, the last King of Burma. I have always remained interested in Burma, and deplored the suffering undergone by the people which still continues, and which will continue until the Generals are got rid of.'

John also recalled hearing about the Indian National Army and he was present at Lord Mountbatten's Victory Parade in Rangoon in June.

8

A family escapes from China to England in 1943

'...The Japanese were coming so we all had to get out of China to avoid ending up in a Japanese concentration camp. We had to leave in a hurry...' Anne

In early 1943 another difficult and dangerous journey was beginning. Marian and Joe Leach now had three young children, Tom, John and Anne. It is difficult to know how close they were to fighting in such a vast country, however there came a point when they decided they must try and get back to England. It was to take them 6 months, travelling by truck, plane, trains and through the Suez Canal on one or possibly two crowded troop ships, with a stay in a camp by the Canal, the worry of a sick child and many moments of risk and hardship. Looking back 70 years, Anne, the youngest writes:

'I was 9 months old when we started the journey home so that would make it early 1943 (I was born in April 1942 in Gweilin).'

Several hundred million years ago this was an area under the sea and the striking mountains with their unique shape that rise steeply out of the water are formed from thousands of years of salt water dissolving and wearing away limestone layers. With a movement of the earth's crust it became land and the isolated limestone peaks developed with wear from wind, rain and rivers. From a boat one can see the wonderful effect of reflections of these peaks rising out of the water.

In April 1942 this part of eastern China was affected by the aftermath of the Doolittle Raid when American pilots were returning from bombing the cities of Tokyo, Nagoya, Yokohama, Yokosuka and Kobe. This was a particularly hazardous air raid when specially trained volunteer pilots flew sixteen modified B-25 bombers that were launched from the U S Navy's aircraft carrier USS Hornet in the Western Pacific in enemy-controlled waters east of Japan.

After a Japanese picket boat spotted the aircraft carrier and sent a warning radio signal to Japan the decision was taken to launch the B-25's 10 hours earlier than previously planned.This meant they had to fly an extra 170 miles. Although huge damage was not inflicted on

Japanese cities the raid significantly improved American morale after Pearl Harbour and raised serious questions about the vulnerability of Japan to air attack.

After the raids when fifteen of the planes flew towards eastern China the weather was getting worse though in fact their speed was increased by a tail wind. However since they had taken off earlier than originally planned they were running low on fuel, so could not reach their intended destination south of Shanghai in Zhejiang province. After thirteen hours of flight all the planes reached the mainland and crash landed or bailed out, and many received help from Chinese soldiers and civilians and John Birch, an American missionary.

All the planes were lost and 67 out of 80 airmen escaped capture and death, though some were either killed or taken prisoner. As a result thousands of Chinese civilians were massacred by the Japanese Army because they gave shelter to surviving American aviators. During searches the Japanese burned Chinese towns and villages, wanting to occupy the area to prevent American air forces from establishing bases from which they could reach the Japanese mainland. They left devastation behind them. Anne writes:

'The Japanese were coming so we all had to get out of China to avoid ending up in a Japanese concentration camp. We had to leave in a hurry - Mum's engagement ring had gone to a jewellers for repair and there was no time to pick it up. Consequently Mum never had an engagement ring, which I always thought strange as a child.
The first part of the journey was in army trucks that had been used to bring Wingate's men somewhere. I was born in Gweilin so presumably we were still near there when we set off. We were driven west across China to somewhere where we got on a rickety aeroplane which flew us over the Himalayas to Calcutta.'

John writes:

'I think Mum said that our journey from Gweilin into western China took 6 weeks by truck. She said it was the Americans who flew us out....'

It is not clear where they flew from, but it may have been Kunming in western China, which was an important Chinese military centre, an American air base and formerly a transport terminus for the Burma

Road (closed between 1942 and January 1945). Kunming is in the middle of the Yunnan-Guizhou Plateau, 6000 feet above sea level.

Around this time there had begun the largest airlift operation in aviation history – it was needed because for nearly three years of the war supplies for China could not be sent along the Burma Road. Many thousands of planes flew 'over the hump' which is between India and Kunming over the eastern Himalayas. They were supporting the U S and the Chinese forces fighting under Chiang Kai-shek.

Flying this route was very hazardous indeed with lack of information about unpredictable weather, violent winds were common and the weight of cargo was often estimated. There was a shortage of experienced pilots, a lack of radio navigation aids and few reliable charts. Various planes were used, but often were not intended for high altitudes so sometimes flew a highly dangerous route through Himalayan mountain passes.

In north east India there were airfields near a section of the India Railways along the Brahmaputra valley – at Chabua the mountains rise quickly to 10,000 feet and higher. The route flying east went over the Patkai Range, then over the upper Chindwin River valley, with the Humon Mountains on the east of 14,000 feet. Then it crossed a series of 14,000 – 16,000 foot ridges and the Santsung Range and approached Kunming.

Only once on December 13 1943 were the strategically important Assam airfields attacked by Japanese bombers, and slight damage was inflicted. The raiders were pursued and then ran into Allied fighter patrols returning from northern Burma.

There was a lot going on in China at this time. The U S Air Force was now engaged in attacks against Japanese inland shipping. After the family had left Gweilin a U S infantry training centre was built there. Between 1943 and 1945 the U S bombed targets such as trains, harbours, railroads in French Indochina and South China, and attacked bridges, oil and gas storage facilities, supply dumps, convoys and enemy troop concentrations. With many commitments to the war effort in other parts of the world the U S's main objective in China was to keep as many Japanese forces engaged as possible so they were less likely to go elsewhere.

The plane that Marian's family flew in may have been a Douglas DC-3 which is an American fixed-wing propeller-driven airliner - this revolutionized air transport in the 1930s and 1940s. During World

War 2 many countries used it for the transport of troops and supplies and many mercy missions and evacuations of prisoners of war.

It is not clear exactly where the family landed in India. Anne writes:

'.....From here we travelled by train across India to Bombay. This took several days, I think.

John writes;

'My very first memories are in India when I would have been 4 years old. They are all just pictures in my memory, one of a large store in Calcutta with an escalator which wondrous machine impressed itself on my young mind; then a scene on the train travelling across India to Bombay when I dropped a toy aeroplane out of the window and lost it.'

By 1929 there was a huge network of railway lines in India, stretching for thousands of miles and reaching most parts of the country. Work had started in the mid 19th century, and by 1880 the network reached the three major port cities of Bombay, Madras and Calcutta, and by 1900 it had spread to Assam, Rajasthan and Andhra Pradesh. In 1907 most of the rail companies were taken over by the government, and soon the first electric locomotive was used, though steam locomotives were not entirely phased out until many years later.

These train journeys for hundreds of miles must have taken many hours. In 1942 Josephine had simply written:

'...May 23rd At 5 am we started the long journey on the train to Calcutta...'

Neither account mentions any disruption or civil unrest they might have experienced on these journeys. However reports of the times suggest that precautions needed to be taken against bandits who could attack at any moment.

There had been considerable turmoil in India. Gandhi had returned to the country in 1915 and wanted Independence and to keep the country together, with Hindus and Moslems continuing to live side by side as they had for many years. And he believed passionately in a non violent response to all wars.

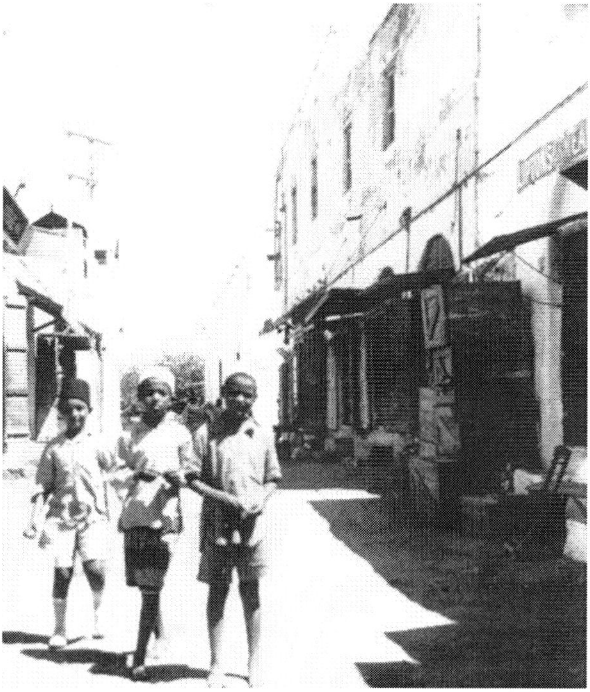

He had transformed the Congress into an organization of the people, with committees all over India, and governing Members were elected with no reference to caste, wealth, ethnicity, religion and sex. They were encouraged to tackle many social and health problems. A new generation of Indian leaders had emerged, including Nehru who later became the first Prime Minister of independent India, and Jinnah who later became Pakistan's first Governor General.

The Congress performed well in the provincial elections of 1937, coming to power in eight of the eleven provinces where elections were held, and there was success in the diversity of political ideologies and optimism about Independence coming soon, though there were also serious differences between different leaders about the future organisation of India.

In October 1939 the British Viceroy, Lord Linlithgow declared British India's entry into the War without consulting the democratically elected Indian leaders. Congress demanded all members resign by the end of the month. However, opinion about the war was divided and Rajagopalachari, the prominent leader from Tamil Nadu resigned from the Congress to actively advocate supporting the British war effort.

And in fact over 2 million Indians volunteered for war service and went on to fight with distinction with the Allies all over the world, and particularly in Asia and North Africa. The Indian Army became the largest all-volunteer force in history. India's production of armaments was vital to the Allies and wealthy Indian princes provided financial assistance.

In 1942 Gandhi wrote to President Roosevelt of what he saw as the hypocrisy of the situation when the Allies claimed to be fighting to make the world safe for the freedom of the individual while at the same time countries like Africa and India were being exploited. Also it is surprising that he wrote to the British Government at the time of the Battle of Britain advocating non violence, to the point of inviting '*Herr Hitler and Signor Mussolini'* to take possession of their island and homes and allowing themselves to be slaughtered. The government replied that the policy which he advocated was one which it was not possible for them to consider.'

One of the aims of the small pro Japanese Indian National Army was to destabilize the British Indian Army and use guerrilla tactics against colonial rule in India. But it lacked manpower and arms and general support.

There was a terrible famine in Bengal between 1940 -43. There were many causes of this linked to the weather conditions and the social and economic upheavals of wartime. In the winter of 1942 some rice crops were hit by a cyclone, three tidal waves and flooding, reserves of food were destroyed and a fungus hit the weakened crops. It is estimated that between 1 and 4 million people died of malnutrition and disease and food prices increased throughout India. Small traders and craftsmen suffered when people had no money to employ them.

The very large city of Calcutta suffered greatly. Bengal had become a food importer, and supplies that would normally have come from Burma were affected by the Japanese occupation, and these problems coincided with an influx of refugees from Burma. Other shipping bringing supplies to the country was hampered by the dangerous situation in the Atlantic and the Japanese presence in the Bay of Bengal.

The main trading route up the river system ceased to operate, putting pressure on the railway system which was already transporting men and equipment to war zones.

In 1942 Gandhi and many thousands of members of Congress who objected to India's involvement in the war were imprisoned, some until the end of the war. Because of failing health Gandhi was released from prison in May 1944 at which point he found that Jinnah's campaign for creating Pakistan had gained much support.

For a short time there was some rioting against the British, some railway stations and post offices were attacked and damaged, telegraph wires were cut and bridges blown up. And there were other problems associated with the war effort. Some trains were diverted to the Middle East, railway workshops were sometimes used as ammunition factories and in places tracks were dismantled for use in the war in other countries. And because of fears of a possible Japanese invasion of India the Army confiscated many boats, motor vehicles, carts and elephants so they would not fall into enemy hands.
Anne writes:

'Once in Bombay we had to wait for a boat to take us to England and as it was wartime the wait was considerable. We were there 6 weeks during which time Tom who must have been about 5 went to school.
I also remember Mum saying that we lived in a sort of cave outside Bombay but I have no idea exactly what she meant...'

John writes:

'Mum also talked of having to provide us children with a milk substitute that she concocted from available ingredients. What the recipe was I don't know but it did include ground up egg shells...'

There are many caves around Mumbai (Bombay) The Elephanta Caves are 6 miles to the east of the city on an island in Mumbai harbour. There are five Hindu caves containing stone sculptures dedicated to the god Shiva, and two Buddhist caves. The architecture of the caves is thought to date back to between the 5th and 8th centuries.

The Jogeshwari Caves in the Mumbai suburb of Jogeshwari are also Hindu and Buddhist temple sculptures of a similar age. The Kanheri Caves are on the western side of Mumbai are now in the forest of the

Sanjay Gandhi National Park. They show the Buddhist influence on the art and culture of India and are carved out of solid black basalt rock. There are other caves which are plainer, with stone plinths for beds, and many have been converted into permanent monasteries. Some caves are used for living, studying and meditating, and are lined with Buddhist sculptures.
Anne writes:

'Eventually we were able to board a boat which was very crowded. I don't know if we travelled all the way to England on the same boat but it went through the Suez canal and I remember Mum saying that we spent quite some time in a refugee camp on the banks of the Suez canal (presumably not on the boat) where John became quite ill and was covered in boils. She found the time on the boat very difficult, I think, for some reason she had to keep us children quiet (discipline wasn't her strong point) and we were of course in constant danger of being torpedoed'.

In November 1942, a few months before they travelled through the Suez Canal there had been the Second Battle of El Alamein, and the Allies' hard won victory marked a turning point in the Western Desert Campaign. It ended the threat that Germany and Italy would take Egypt, the Suez Canal and gain access to the Middle East oilfields. The situation had been hugely improved with the arrival in the Western Desert of Sherman tanks, 6-pounder anti-tank guns and Spitfires. Some of Churchill's most famous words were said about this moment – it was not the end, it was not even the beginning of the end. But it was, perhaps, the end of the beginning.

John writes:

' ...on passage through Suez seeing gunnery practise where the guns, I think on our ship, shot up an empty rowing boat. When we finally arrived in Liverpool Dad had no money for the train fare to Bradford, which was where his parents lived, and he had to borrow it from the station master.'

In August 1944 after battles in Hunan and Guangdong the Imperial Japanese Army launched attacks on Gweilin where the family had started their journey. Most civilians had fled and after 10 days of intense fighting the Japanese occupied the city and were in control of two thirds of Guangxi province. Thousands of civilians were killed and wounded. The aim was to connect Japanese held territory and destroy American air bases. This was one of the most devastating losses for China in the war against the invading Japanese.

9

The beginning of the end

"....We do not intend that the Japanese shall be enslaved as a race or destroyed as a nation,...' (The Potsdam Declaration, July1945, issued by Winston Churchill President Truman and the Chairman of the Nationalist Government of China, Chiang Kai-shek.)

THE ADVANCE OF THE ALLIES DOWN THROUGH BURMA

Some of the places Josephine travelled through in Burma 1942 are mentioned in accounts of the Burma Campaign of 1944/5 – Indaw, Sagaing, Shwebo, Pakokku and Myingyan, Mandalay and Pegu. The British 26th Division advanced southwards down the valley of the Railway toward Indaw. The Chinese New First Army advanced from Myitkyina to Bhamo. The Japanese held on in the Sagaing hills while they tried to delay the Allies advance near the Irrawaddy River.

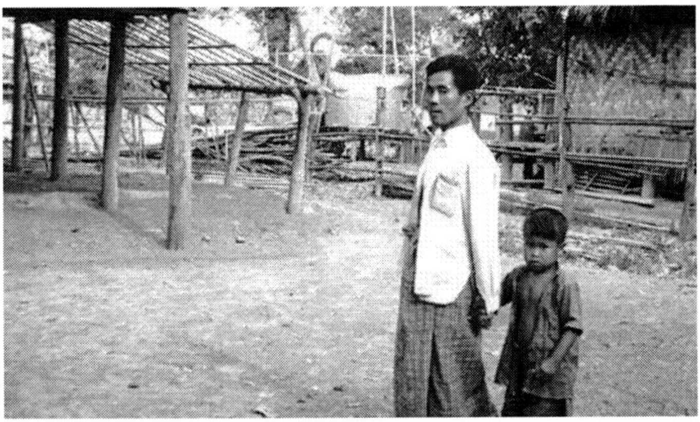

Large amounts of supplies were flown in by the Allies and projects were undertaken to improve the land route from India into Burma. Units from the 14th Army crossed the Chindwin River and attacked into the Shwebo plain, and later other units aimed to cross the Irrawaddy close to Pakokku. It was the dry season and the mechanized brigades could move rapidly in the open countryside. Indian divisions captured the important river port at Myingyan.

Though Mandalay was taken by an Indian division on 20th March, the Japanese held on for some days to the Royal Palace and many old buildings were burned to the ground. When the city was finally re-taken the Allies were greeted by crowds of cheering local people.

Some parties of Japanese soldiers made their way east into the Shan States. It was vital for the Allies to recapture Rangoon before the monsoon began as the reconstructed overland routes from India would become waterlogged and flying operations would be strongly affected. Karen forces delayed the Japanese who were trying to block the road to Rangoon. There were various attacks on Toungoo from where the Japanese were finally driven back.

A Japanese division blocked the advance to Pegu using anti-tank mines improvised from aircraft bombs, anti-aircraft guns and suicide attacks, but were eventually driven to the hills to the west. The monsoon broke and floods slowed the advance.

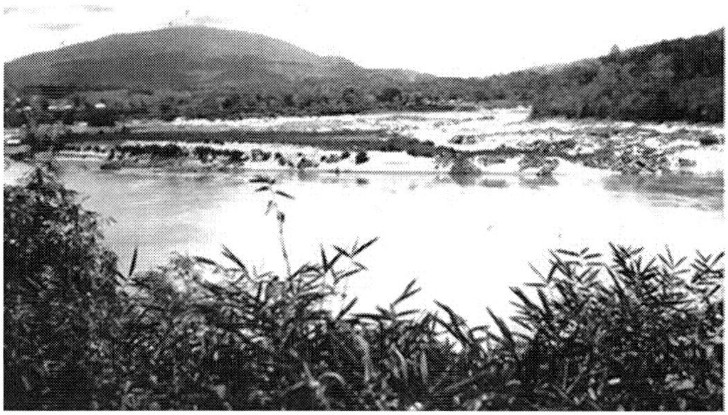

In the original plan to re-take Burma an amphibious assault had been intended to be carried out before the army reached the capital, but it had been postponed.

However the Japanese were evacuating Rangoon, some going by sea. On May 1st a Gurkha parachute battalion was dropped on Elephant Point and cleared the remaining Japanese rearguards from the mouth of the Rangoon River, and Indian forces landed the next day and took over Rangoon.

Lord Mountbatten held a victory parade in Rangoon on June 15th despite the fact that thousands of Japanese were still fighting behind British lines and many were trying to move across the Sittang river back into Thailand. The Burma Road was re-opened so again supplies could be sent to Nationalist China.

Some Japanese troops were still in control of Tenasserim in the south and some were cut off in a range of low jungle-covered hills between the Irrawaddy and Sittang rivers. Some fighting took place in flooded countryside. Many perished trying to cross the swollen Sittang river on improvised rafts.

THE CALL FOR JAPAN TO SURRENDER

Potsdam is a beautiful city with lakes, parks and palaces situated on the River Havel, 15 miles southwest of Berlin. It was a city where Prussian Kings and German Kaisers lived until 1918. In 1933 in Potsdam's Garrison Church there had been a ceremonial handshake between President Paul von Hindenburg and the new Chancellor Adolf Hitler in what became known as the "Day of Potsdam" – this symbolized the beginning of Hitler's Third Reich.

By 1945 Potsdam had suffered severe war damage and Berlin lay in ruins. On April 30, with the Battle of Berlin raging above him, Hitler had committed suicide in his bunker. Following the unconditional surrender of Nazi Germany on 8 May (V-E Day) the Potsdam Conference took place from July 17th to August 2nd in the stunningly beautiful Cecilienhof Palace close to the Jungfernsee Lak. This was the last palace built by the Hohenzollern family. Emperor Wilhelm II of Germany had it erected for his son, Crown Prince Wilhelm of Germany, and the crown prince's wife Duchess Cecilie of Mecklenburg-Schwerin.

Churchill, Clement Attlee, the new U S President Truman and Stalin met to decide the future of Germany and postwar Europe and they produced the Potsdam Agreement. In addition on July 26, Truman, Churchill, and the Chairman of the Nationalist Government of China, Chiang Kai-shek issued the Potsdam Declaration, which outlined the terms of surrender for the Empire of Japan. The leaders at the conference were already aware of the existence of the new atom bomb but this was not specifically mentioned in the Declaration.

This ultimatum stated that, if Japan did not surrender, it would face "prompt and utter destruction."

It contained the warning

"We will not deviate from them. There are no alternatives. We shall brook no delay."

For Japan the terms were:

the elimination "for all time of the authority and influence of those who have deceived and misled the people of Japan into embarking on world conquest"
the occupation of "points in Japanese territory to be designated by the Allies"
"Japanese sovereignty shall be limited to the islands of Honshu, Hokkaido, Kyushu, Shikoku and such minor islands as we determine." As had been announced in the Cairo Declaration in 1943.
"The Japanese military forces shall be completely disarmed"
"stern justice shall be meted out to all war criminals, including those who have visited cruelties upon our prisoners"

The declaration also said:

"We do not intend that the Japanese shall be enslaved as a race or destroyed as a nation, ... The Japanese Government shall remove all obstacles to the revival and strengthening of democratic tendencies among the Japanese people. Freedom of speech, of religion, and of thought, as well as respect for the fundamental human rights shall be established."

"Japan shall be permitted to maintain such industries as will sustain her economy and permit the exaction of just reparations in kind, but not those which would enable her to rearm for war. To this end, access to, as distinguished from control of, raw materials shall be permitted. Eventual Japanese participation in world trade relations shall be permitted."

"The occupying forces of the Allies shall be withdrawn from Japan as soon as these objectives have been accomplished and there has been established, in accordance with the freely expressed will of the Japanese people, a peacefully inclined and responsible government."

The only mention of "unconditional surrender" came at the end of the declaration:

" We call upon the government of Japan to proclaim now the unconditional surrender of all Japanese armed forces, and to provide proper and adequate assurances of their good faith in such action. The alternative for Japan is prompt and utter destruction."

The declaration made no direct mention of the Emperor. It did, however, insist that

"the authority and influence of those who have deceived and misled the people of Japan into embarking on world conquest must be eliminated for all time".

Allied intentions on issues of utmost importance to the Japanese, including whether Hirohito was to be regarded as one of those who had "misled the people of Japan" or even a war criminal, or alternatively whether the Emperor might potentially become part of a "peacefully inclined and responsible government" were left unresolved.

The ultimatum was broadcast to the Japanese Home Islands on the radio while leaflets describing it were dropped by American bombers. Prime Minister Suzuki met the Japanese press and confirmed his government's commitment to fight on.

As a result the decision was taken to drop atom bombs on the Japanese cities of Hiroshima and Nagasaki on the 6th and 9th of August 1945. The destruction was on a scale beyond anything human beings had experienced before in wartime. On August 15th Japan finally surrendered and the documents were signed on the deck of the American battleship USS Missouri on September 2nd 1945.

At Taukkyan War Cemetery 25 kilometres north of Rangoon are the graves of 6,374 soldiers who died in World War 2, the graves of 52 soldiers from World War l, and memorial pillars with the names of over 27,000 Commonwealth soldiers including many Indian and African soldiers who died in World War ll and have no known grave.

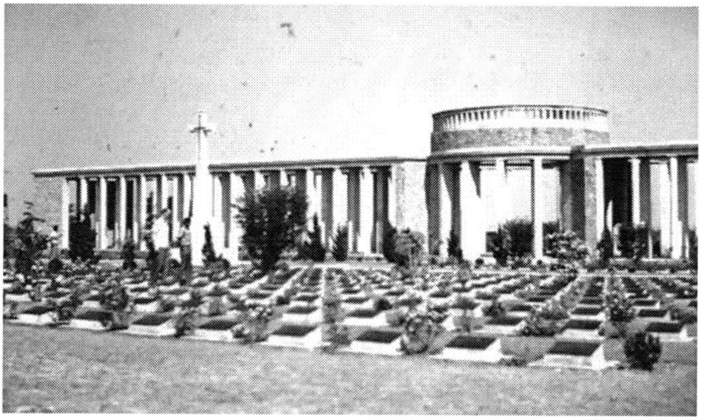

Five holders of the Victoria Cross are buried here.
Also inscribed on the Rangoon Memorial in English, Hindi, Urdu, Gurmukhi, and Burmese are the words

They died for all free men

10
Independence, a bullet in a bible and a baby in a drawer

...Our house was in the front line and we had to be evacuated at 20 minutes notice. Now our house has been looted and we possess practically nothing....' Josephine

AUNG SAN

General Aung San 1915 – 1947, the father of Aung Sang Suu Kyi, was a nationalist and co founder of the modern Burmese Army and the Communist Party of Burma. He worked towards Burma's independence but was assassinated six months before it was achieved in 1948. In the final stages of the war Aung San's Burmese National Army (which had decided not to support Japan any further) had given valuable help to the 14th Army which was made up of Indians, Africans and the British.

After being educated at a Buddhist monastic school, and a high school he became politically active while studying at Rangoon University. In 1938 he became a Thakin which means a master and lord in his own country. He also helped found another nationalist organization called the Freedom Bloc which was an alliance between politically active monks and the Poor Man's Party.

In March 1940 shortly before the Japanese invasion of Burma, he went to the Indian National Congress Assembly and the British government in Burma issued a warrant for his arrest because of what they regarded as his revolutionary activities. He went to China and then Japan. In 1943 when Japan declared Burma to be an 'independent nation' Aung San was appointed War Minister but he became sceptical of Japan's intentions and ability to win the war and made contact with the British authorities in India. On 27 March 1945, he led the Burmese National Army in a revolt against the Japanese occupiers.

The patriotic Burmese Forces were later disbanded and Aung San was offered a position in the Burma Army under British command, but instead he became a civilian political leader and military leader of the People's Volunteer Organisation.

Bishop West wrote an account of how after the war General Aung San came to Kappali followed by large crowds and was greeted by Khay Mah, Taw Mwa, Ko Tha Dun, Ta Preh Paw and fellow Christians.

Kappali church

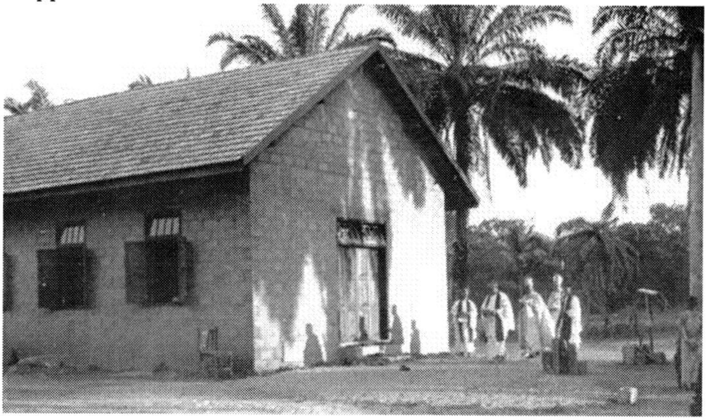

The British still regarded him as subversive and on May 18, 1946 the PVO and the Communist Party organized a demonstration in the streets of Tantabin (north of Rangoon). The police opened fire and killed 3 people and more than 40 were injured.

Aung San became President of the Anti Fascist People's Freedom League and was made Deputy Chairman of the Executive Council of Burma by the newly appointed British Governor, Sir Hubert Rance who had a more accepting attitude than the previous Governor, recognising the support Aung San had from the Burmese people.

It has been suggested that discussions about the future of Burma at this stage omitted to take into account all the hopes of various ethnic minorities, and it could be said that the British failed to give this question sufficient attention. In the agreement signed in London in January 1947 by the British Prime Minister Clement Attlee and Aung San, none of the ethnic minority groups were mentioned. Aung San was uncompromising in his wish for complete independence outside membership of the Commonwealth. In the following month at the Panglong Conference when an agreement was signed between Aung

San and Shan, Kachin and Chin leaders expressing solidarity for a united Burma, there were other groups who were not consulted such as the Karens, the Mon and the Arakanese. In the General Elections in April 1947 the AFPFL won 176 out of 210 seats with Karens winning 24, the Communists 6 and Anglo-Burmans 4. In July Aung San arranged meetings in Rangoon to discuss the rehabilitation of Burma.

Later that month this political process was seriously affected by the assassination of Aung San together with six of his cabinet ministers. A report of the time states:

'1947; July, 19: General Aung San, acclaimed Burmese nationalist harbinger since his student years in the 1930s, veteran of the 'Thirty Comrades' and revered hero of Burma's independent struggle was assassinated in Rangoon's Secretariat, along with his elder brother and six cabinet ministers. The circumstances of the event now known as 'Martyrs' Day' still remain unclear, even though radical military factions as well as a few rival political leaders and even the British secret services were suspected culprits.'

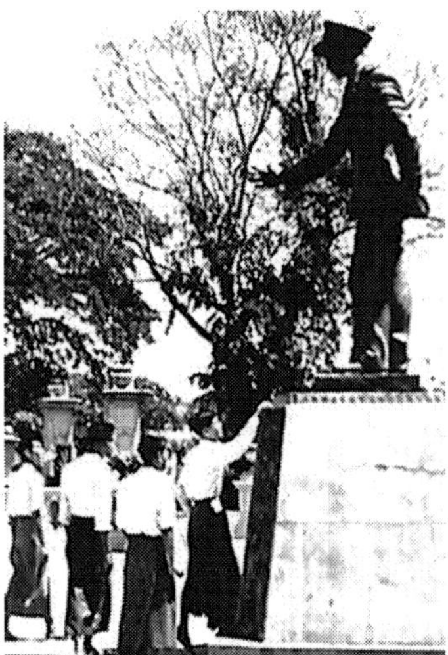

He is a national hero and is revered as the architect of Burmese Independence. This statue stands beside Lake Kandawgyi in Rangoon.

A cafe in 2012

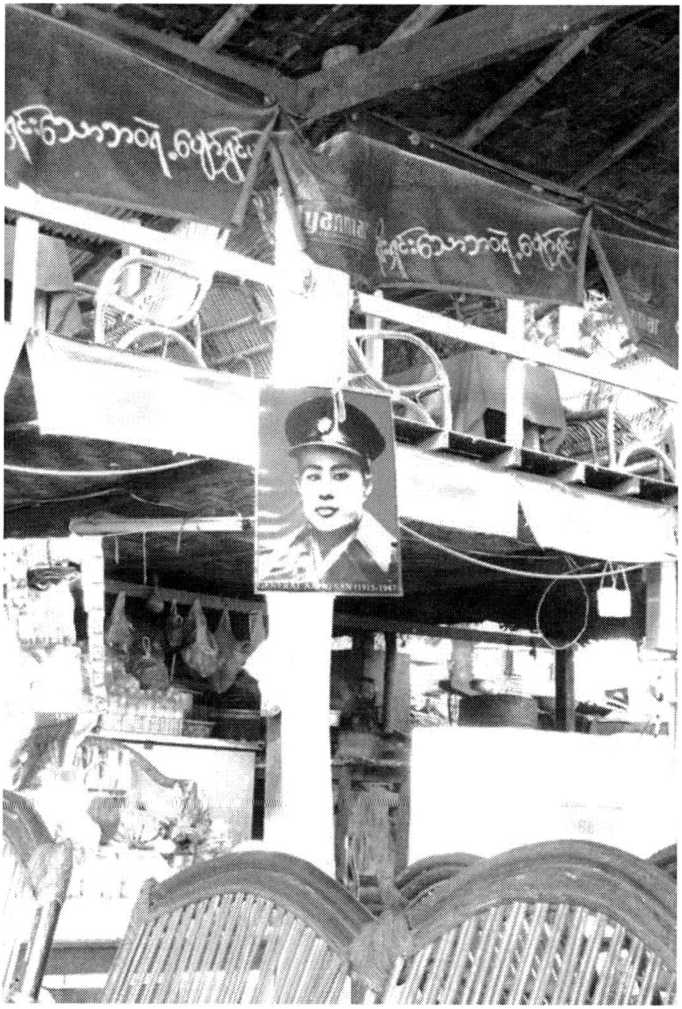

MORE EVENTS IN 1947

In 1947 much attention was focused on India and the upheavals and bloodshed that followed the dividing of the country into India and Pakistan. The British Labour government promised independence to the two opposing factions, the Indian National Congress and the Muslim League because of the threat of civil war and the mutiny of the Royal Indian Navy during 1946. Lord Louis Mountbatten was appointed the last Viceroy of India and was under pressure to find a solution - many people were displaced and as they travelled to new areas fighting broke out on a huge scale and thousands of lives were lost.

In November 1947, ten years after her sister Marian married Joe Leach in Shanghai, Josephine Chapman married Christopher Lewis in Rangoon Cathedral. They moved to Maymyo. The church seen here still stands today.

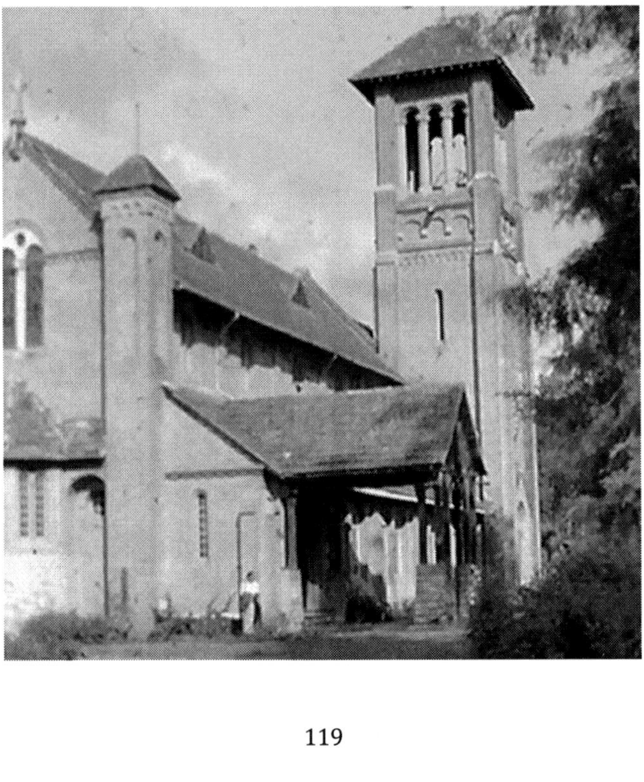

Josephine wrote a book for children about these years. Stories give brief impressions of life in Burma during and after the war. She described the vivid colours, the trees called *'Flame of the Forest'* and the *'Gold Mohur'*. There was... *the Padauk which is very curious. It has a pretty small yellow blossom which comes three times, but which lasts only for one day each time. "The Padauk blossom is out" someone will say, and then everybody goes to see it, because they know that it will be dead by the next morning....'The forests also are full of beautiful birds, peacocks and parrots and many others.....*

'Each monk may only have eight things which he calls his own: three pieces of yellow cloth which make his robe, his girdle, his begging-bowl, a razor to shave his head, a needle to mend his clothes, and a water-strainer...'

In the diary she had mentioned the disruption of many schools in January 1942, including the one at Kemmendine. This had been started by William Jackson, a blind priest from South London who travelled to Burma, learnt Burmese and built the school...

'There was one day when the blind boys of Kemmendine were taken to sing in Rangoon Cathedral, and even people in England can hear them because somebody came once and made a gramophone record of their singing. During the war when the Japanese came to Rangoon, all the blind boys had to go home to their villages. But their school and St Michael's church were not destroyed, and now they are beginning to come back again......They washed and repainted St Michael's Church and built a new Altar, for the old one had been destroyed by the Japanese....'

She described a very tiny hospital run by Avice Cam in the Delta.

'...One good thing about a one-roomed house is that you can see through the windows in every direction while you are sitting at your meals. On one side there is the river, sparkling in the morning sunlight; on the other, as far as the eye can see, there stretch the green rice-fields; in front, one can see the pathway along the river bank with shady bamboos and little houses beside it; and behind, through a doorway, one can see a covered stairway and passage leading to the little hospital beyond.....but when the Japanese came to Burma.......they burnt down the little hospital and Miss

Cam's house, and the bamboo landing-stage; and there are no medicines left in the villages.....'

She described how Burmese people were used for forced labour, building roads and railways and tunnels, and that the Japanese often stole the bullocks and water buffalo which were so essential for the cultivation of the land.

There is a little story:

'In a little village called Kyonmago east of the great Salween river there lives a Chinaman called U Kin Ma. He is about eighty years old and he had four sons and one daughter, and twenty-two grandchildren. I think he is the richest man in the village, and he lives in quite a big house. He was a trader, and now his sons are traders too, and before the war all his grandchildren went to high school in the town. ...one day during the war time evil men came to his village and called him from his house. "You are a Christian," they said. "Yes," U Kin Ma replied......"Then you must be a friend of the British and an enemy of the Japanese. You must be a spy." "I am not a spy. I live quietly in the village," he replied. "All Christians are spies," the men said, "And because you are a Christian, we are going to kill you." The old man smiled at them, not frightened at all. "I am an old man," he said, "And there is not much more work I can do for Jesus Christ. Soon I shall die in any case. So it does not matter if you kill me now. In fact I shall be glad to die for my Master Jesus." The evil men were very surprised at his reply.. They did not like him for being a Christian, but they knew that he was a very brave man to answer like that,.... So they did not kill him, and soon after they went away from the village. U Kin Ma is still living there now that the war is finished.'

'Aeroplanes flew over the villages and dropped not bombs, but small pieces of paper, and when the people picked them up and read what was written on them, they were very excited and happy. "The British are coming back soon," they read. They did not have to wait very long before the whole of Burma was freed from the Japanese..... but during the war roads, railways and bridges had been destroyed, and there were very few boats and trains, so it was still very difficult for people to travel from place to place....'

She described how a Bishop was lent a plane by the RAF and flew over a village dropping a bundle of letters which landed in the garden of a monastery. They were found and distributed to people who were isolated and unable to get news.

1948 – BURMESE INDEPENDENCE

On Jan. 4th 1948 the Union of Burma was created with Sao Shwe Thaik as its first President and U Nu its first Prime Minister. A Parliament was formed made up of a Chamber of Deputies and a Chamber of Nationalities. Here is an extract from a newspaper article Jan 4th, 1948.

'...At 4.20 this morning, an hour chosen by Burmese astrologers as the most auspicious for the birth of a new republic, the guns of the cruiser HMS Birmingham crashed out a celebration of the independence of the Union of Burma.

While the guns were sounding their message, a large group of statesmen and diplomats gathered somewhat sleepily at the Secretariat, Burma's Houses of Parliament, for the ceremony of lowering the Union Jack and hoisting the national flag of Burma.

As the Union Jack was slowly lowered, star shells burst overhead, church bells rang throughout Rangoon and rifle volleys were fired by jubilant Burmese soldiers. The city is to give itself over to celebration for the next five days.'

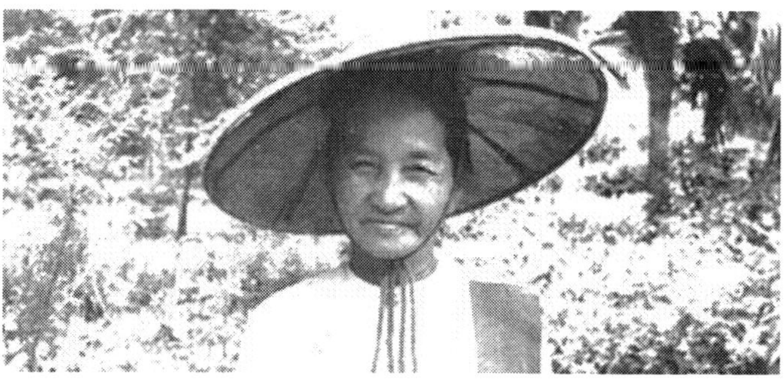

‘MASTER SWEET SMILING’
Jo and Christopher had their first child, David in September 1948.

Maymyo

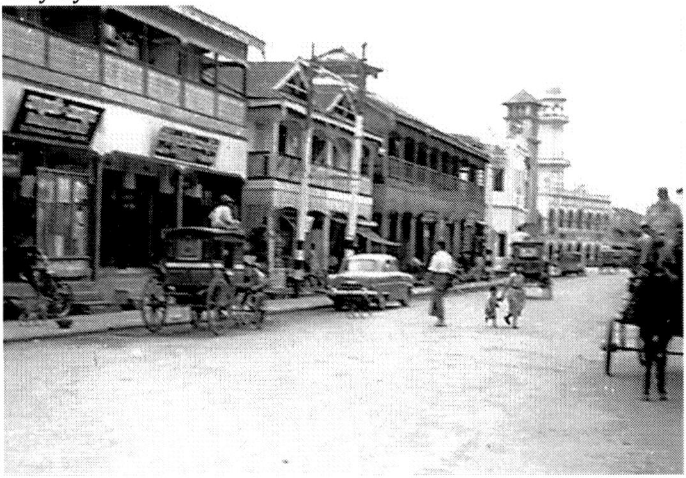

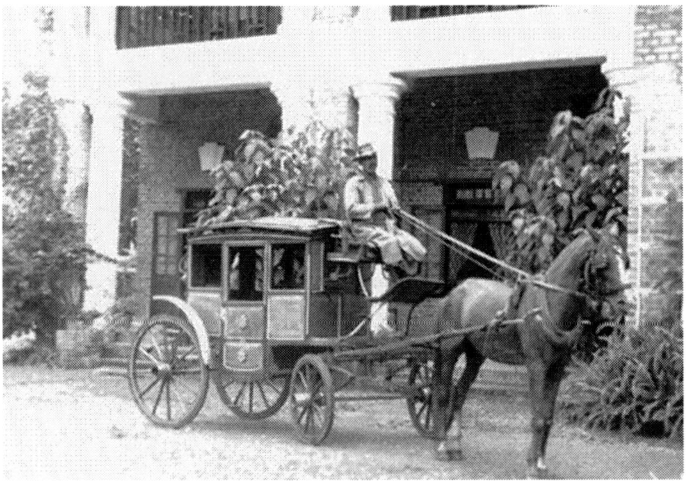

There are some letters Jo wrote to Annie Chapman, her own mother in England:

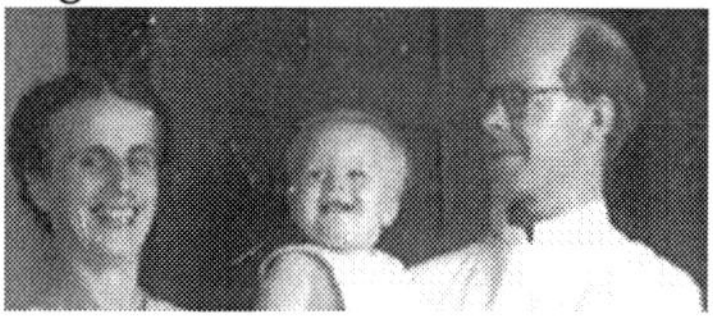

The Parsonage, Maymyo
28/10/48 '......Our climate here in Maymyo is ideal for babies....'

'....He lies naked in the sun for five minutes at 9 a.m. each day with only his head shaded from the sun under the pram hood, and he spends the rest of the day outside in the shade. On the other hand it is not hot enough in Maymyo for him to get prickly heat as all babies do in the plains....'

'06/12/48 The Metropolitan of India from Calcutta has come to Rangoon and Christopher has gone to Rangoon to meet him. I hope he will bring back some baby food for David. We are getting into difficulties about that because the Burma Government has stopped all imports of it and it is nearly sold out. Somebody searched the bazaar in Mandalay for me the other day and found three small tins of 'Cow and Gate'. I have enough to last to the middle of January, so I hope Christopher manages to get hold of some in Rangoon.'

'22/12/48 Christopher wrote*: I am just back from Rangoon, and the most important event of my going, in Josephine's eyes at least, is that I have brought back 12 large tins of baby food at their correct price – half that we should have had to pay in Maymyo.*

During the months after independence there were reports of civil disturbances. Some Karens held leading positions in the government and the army and attempted to live peacefully with the Burman ethnic majority. But conflict developed between minority groups and armed militias under the control of General Ne Win.

A report of the times states:

'....the newly nominated Prime Minister, U Nu, failed to maintain the cohesion of the country, which rapidly collapsed into a protracted civil war. Political and ethnic insurgencies took up arms against each other (Communist, Arakanese, Naga, Karen, Karenni,Mon...), threatening the stability of the decolonized country, ethnic Burman militias killed at least 80 Karen villagers near Palaw (southern Burma), by throwing hand grenades into a church on Christmas Eve. Several similar incidents led by local armed militias occurred during the following days until the end of January 1949, hundreds of Karen insurgents mined a train near Mandalay, killing 30 passengers'.

When David was 6 months old in March 1949 the domestic details in the letters are interrupted. Fighting was suddenly all around them.

08/03/49 A very hasty note for I have an opportunity of sending it in the Embassy mail bag and the Consul's wife is off to Rangoon by air in a few minutes. We are staying at the Consul's house....our house was in the front line and we had to be evacuated at 20 minutes notice. Now our house has been looted and we possess practically nothing, though I did manage to take all David's food with me and we have enough for two months. We did not manage to bring his cot, so he sleeps in the bottom drawer of a chest of drawers. We are well and David is quite unperturbed and went on having his feed one afternoon with mortar bombs falling just up the hill.

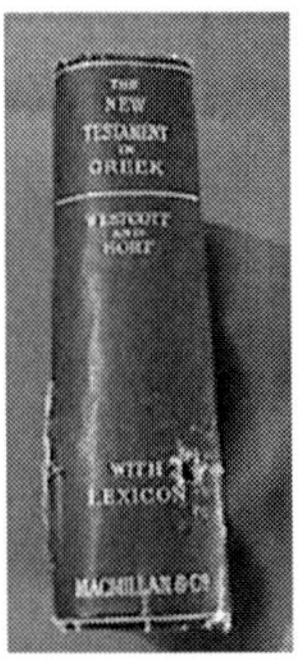

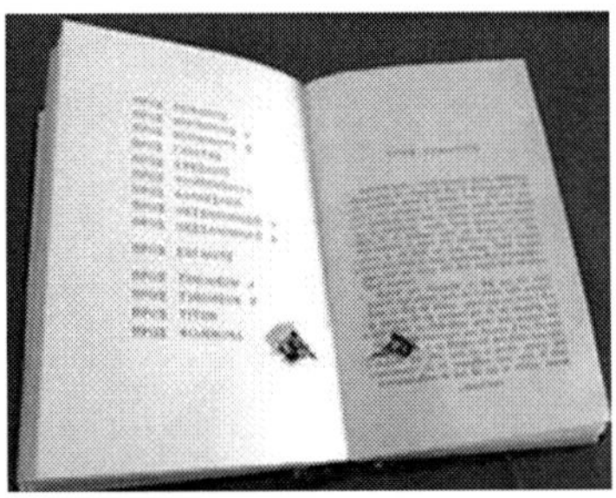

At one point Christopher was in great danger. He was sitting at his desk when a bullet was fired through the window in his study, whizzed passed his head and embedded itself in a bible. This was the New Testament in Greek which he read all his life, seeking the truest meaning he could from the texts that inspired his faith.

They were just in time to get on the last evacuation plane with very few belongings.

Cathedral Parsonage, Rangoon
13/03/49 We are now at the Cathedral Parsonage in Rangoon. Most of the All Saints' congregation in Maymyo left when the troubles there began and it looked as if Christopher was going to be left without any work. Meanwhile the Cathedral Chaplain has had to go home on sick leave and so the Bishop sent a message through to the Embassy that C was to come to Rangoon. So we were just in time to get on the last evacuation plane leaving Maymyo. The journey took 2 ½ hours. David thoroughly enjoyed himself, slept part of the way and talked and laughed to himself the rest of the time. He certainly is a good baby. Apart from David's food and clothes and pram, we have practically nothing and are more or less in the state we were in when we left Burma in 1942.

The only shade we could find at the airport in Mingaladon to put David's cot while waiting for transport into Rangoon was the wing of the aeroplane. Now the poor child is covered in prickly heat and does not like the change from Maymyo at all.'

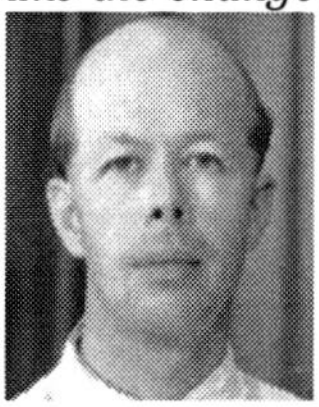

They lost Jo's wedding dress and Christopher's violin, and his ordination certificate from 1932. On a copy certificate which he received later from Bishop West there is a handwritten note in the bottom corner which says: *'the original was lost in the civil disturbance in Maymyo, Burma in March 1949'.*

27/03/49 David is flourishing and getting used to the heat, but it is quite complicated to look after a baby in this sort of climate. He has to be put inside the mosquito net without letting any mosquitoes in and at 10p.m. when he is taken up for his feed they are fairly buzzing around. The legs of his cot have to stand in bowls of water so that ants cannot get into his bed (if he dribbled or was the slightest bit sick, the ants would be on to it in no time.) I have to rub him all over with calamine lotion two or three times in the heat of the day to prevent him from getting prickly heat. However he is surviving and spends the greater part of the day laughing and the greater part of the night sleeping.
Burmese friends in Rangoon say he looks like his father, but he has learnt to laugh from his mother. They nicknamed him, the English meaning – 'Master sweet smiling'.

01/05/49 When it is raining he takes his walk up and down the aisles of the Cathedral and loves to watch the sparrows which Christopher and the Cathedral Council are doing their best to get rid of. On Sunday mornings and on weekdays I sometimes take him and leave him at the Cathedral door while I go to Church, and he can be heard from inside laughing at the birds in the eaves.

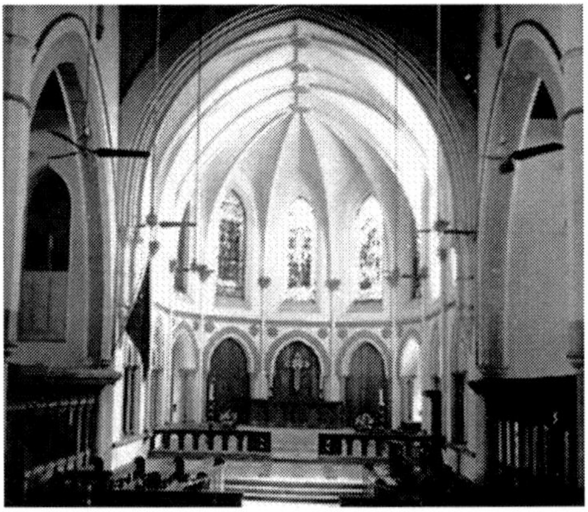

It sounds like they felt safe from civil unrest for the time being. During these months Christopher worked on restoration projects in Rangoon Cathedral creating a Forces Chapel and Burma Chapel.

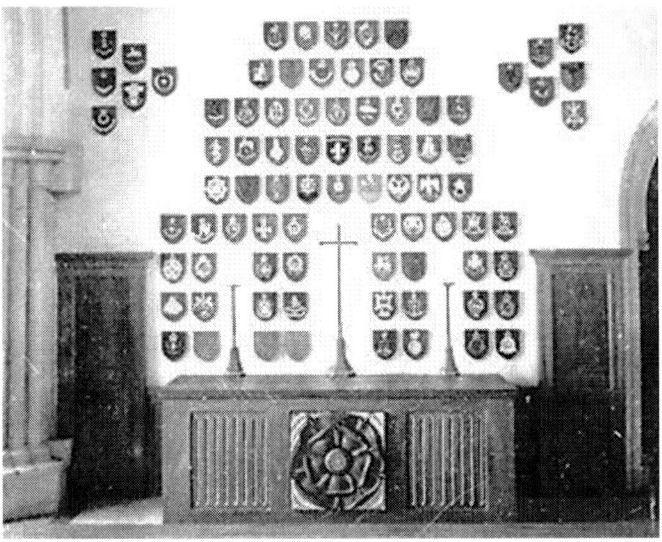

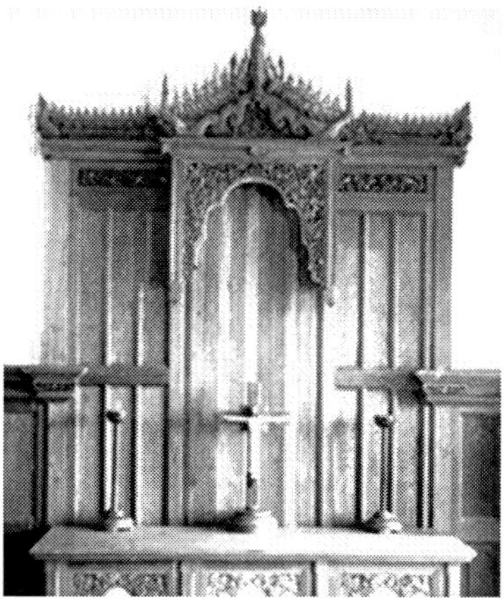

There is a letter Bishop George West wrote in December:

My Dear Christopher

May I congratulate you on the way in which all your preparation for the Cathedral Mission has been crowned with success? I have been wanting for some time to express my appreciation to you for the gifted way you have been adding to our Cathedral these two beautiful memorial chapels.

As the debt to you both for the Mission and for the chapels is due from the Diocese as well as the Cathedral parish it gives me great pleasure to appoint you an honorary Canon of the Cathedral of the Holy Trinity, Rangoon.

I hope you will allow the Diocese as well as myself personally the satisfaction of knowing your good work has not gone without some outward expression of gratitude. This satisfaction will be shared by our friends at home no less than by our friends out here.

In all events I can think of no better way of expressing an appreciation and gratitude than by offering you this canonry

With my best wishes Yours affectionately
+George Rangoon

There is a moving story of a visit from a Japanese sailor.

30/01/50 A few days ago we had a visit from a Japanese sailor from the first Japanese ship to come to Rangoon since the end of the war. In his broken and inadequate English he made us understand that he was a Christian and the Japanese Christians were not at war with us and were sorry for the damage his country had done to Burma. He played with David and they got on very well together, their standard of English being about the same!

He came again the next day with a quaint letter written by a sailor friend to explain more adequately what he wanted to say.

Please beg your pardon the other yesterday. that time I canno
speak English very sorry, I judged only ~~the~~ yours
and came back to my ship. I remember that visited time.
When I Hoped with precher I ~~thank you~~ don't know ~~th~~ How to thank you.
I supposed ~~that~~ inside the heaven My Heart is very pleasant.
When I come back to Japan, speak to my friend and Japanese
precher that Burma people and church's people is very
Kindly. and also. I speak to ~~the~~ sunday school's childre
Not fail. In Japanese people very pleasant
First time came to Rangoon I found out the Kindness people
~~That~~ Before time I want to thank you very much, but I don't speak
to you in English and Then I want to thank you in this letter.
Japan and Burma must be stand in 1 hand in futher.
my ship Leaving this port yesterday. and Then came back
to Japan I get down from this ship for next month.
I have no house and no parents and brother and
Sister. Only one man in the world. I am thinking every
time that my father is Jesus christ. and came back Japan
I live in moji ~~church~~ church
If you sent to me a letter please sent to following adress.
my adress.
Yoshio Hayase
c/o Daiju Kirihara
4th street Saiwaimachi moji Japan.
Please sent to me a letter I sent to you a letter, too.
I don't forget you Kindness Not fail. good bye good
bye. my frien countr~~yes~~ies precher
I Hope your health and your happiness.
Good bye once more say!!

Toshio Hayase

Here is a transcription:

*'Please beg your pardon the other yesterday. that time I cannot speak English very sorry, I judged only your (*word left out?)....... *and came back to my ship. I remember that visited time. When I (*hoped*?) with preacher I don't know how to thank you. I supposed that rise to the heaven. My heart is very pleasant. When I come back to Japan, speak to my friend and Japanese preacher that Burma people and church's people is very kindly and also I speak to Sunday school's children. Not fail. In Japanese people very pleasant.*

First time came to Rangoon I found out the kindness people. Before time I want to thank you very much. But I don't speak to you in English and then I want to thank you in this letter. Japan and Burma must be hand in hand in further.

My ship leaving this port yesterday, and then came back to Japan. I get down from this ship for next month. I have no house and no parents and brother and sister. Only one man in the world. I am thinking every time that my father is Jesus Christ. And came back Japan I live in Moji church. (he gave his address)

..please sent to me a letter I sent to you a letter too. I don't forget you kindness not fail..Good bye good bye my (foreign?) *country's preacher. And I hope your health and your happiness. Good bye once more say!!*

Toshio Hayase

He sat in silence while we read the letter and then he unfolded a bright green silk scarf and handed us a book of Fra Angelico pictures in colour which he informed us he had had since he was a little boy and that he wanted to give it to David. We were reluctant to accept what was obviously a treasure to him, but could do nothing else. Fortunately we had a book of pictures of the Madonna and Child by Old Masters, also in colour, and so we made him a present in return. He wrapped it up in his green silk scarf and off he went.

19/05/50 At last we have managed to arrange a little holiday and we are in Taung-gyi, a hill station of 5,000 feet in the Shan States...I thought David would be frightened in the aeroplane, but he was quite fascinated and enjoyed it all and was very good...David is getting a good colour and is fatter than ever. He is enjoying too the cows and ducks and chickens that he does not see in Rangoon. Last night he lay awake for quite an hour because there were four fireflies in his bedroom. It is amazing the amount of light they give out in a dark room. He keeps on exclaiming to himself, 'There it is!' He is beginning to talk quite a lot

The Shan States (photo 2012)

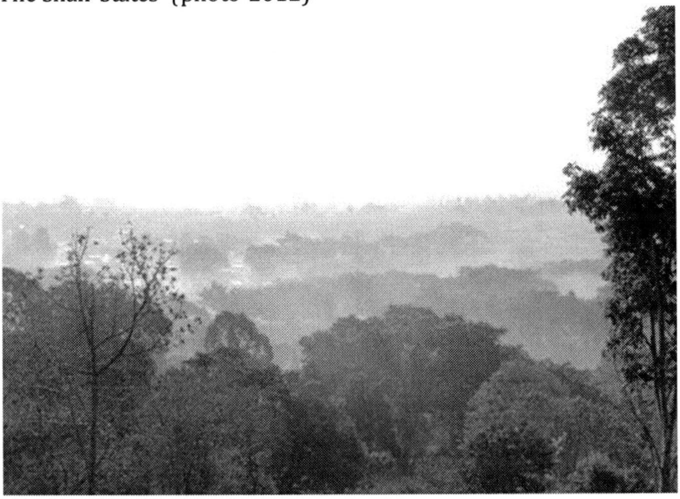

In April 1942 she had written: *'... The Shan States are beautiful and ideal for a touring holiday....'*

29/05/50 The monsoon has broken and so we had rather a bumpy journey back to Rangoon. I was sick though David and Christopher did not mind at all and thoroughly enjoyed it. It certainly was very interesting, passing over and under and through rain clouds and we saw several rainstorms, first one side of us and then the other, though the pilot quite cleverly avoided passing through rain all the way. We are all feeling better for the holiday and David has quite rosy cheeks, an unusual sight in Rangoon. Unfortunately he will not keep them for long. He is getting quite fast with his walking and says a number of things quite clearly. On the return journey when we were weighed for the aeroplane he weighed 27lbs. and I weighed 8 stones 3lbs.

There are worries and difficulties looking after a baby in the climate. After he was born his weight had gone down to 5lb 12 oz.

19/06/50 David has been having his worst teething attack. He also had an attack of bronchitis and I had to take him to the doctor who is treating him with liniment and mixtures and what not. He is still coughing a lot though he has had no fever. I expect it is partly due to this damp house we live in. The long open verandas are an advantage for the heat, but they are a nuisance in the rains. They face west and so the monsoon rain which comes from the south-west beats in and they are under water most of the time. But you can't get from one room to another without going out on to the veranda, and sometimes when one goes upstairs (especially if one is taking David) one needs an umbrella. So it is a little difficult to know how to keep an active toddler dry all the season. Last year the problem did not arise, because he had not got beyond the playpen stage. However I suppose we shall survive. David also had an anti-diphtheria injection the other day, but has had no reaction whatever as far as I can see. There are lots of coughs and colds in Rangoon at present, and some whooping cough.

26/06/50 Yesterday I found him clasping one of his hands in the other and saying: 'How do you do? How do you do?' He can also count up to six, which seems to me pretty good, though of course I have no other child to compare him with, and I suppose everybody thinks their own child is wonderful!

04/07/50 I am sorry to say that David now has whooping cough. There is some of it about in Rangoon, but I can't think of any case he has been in contact with. He remains cheerful in between whiles, but the spasms are pretty awful. The poor little soul knows sometimes when they are coming on and cries, but of course they have to come. The worrying thing is that he cannot keep down any food to speak of and he has lost a pound in weight in under a week. He has to have a series of four injections spread over two weeks and he has had one of them. I hope they will help to shorten the attack. He has rather disturbed nights too of course and is getting overtired from lack of a long stretch of sleep.

07/02/51 David keeps telling people he is going to England to see

Grandma, but he obviously had not the faintest idea of what it meant, for one day he added: 'Grandma's on the table and goes round and round.' He was thinking of the gramophone! However, now he says he is going to England to have dinner in Grandma's house.

This letter is the only information available about their return home. They decided to travel on a ship to England, leaving Burma for the time being and not knowing that it would soon become inaccessible for many years.

RETURN TO CHINA

After 1945 Joe Leach went back to China for several years. The civil war continued until 1949 when the The People's Republic of China was established under Mao Tse-Tung.

On this old photo is written: *'Gweilin Christians at the reopening of rebuilt women's missionaries house, 1946. First house destroyed by Japanese bombers'*

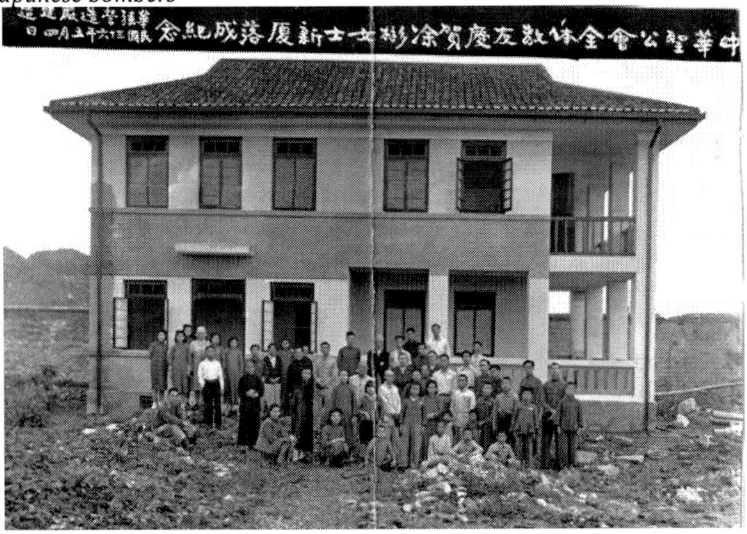

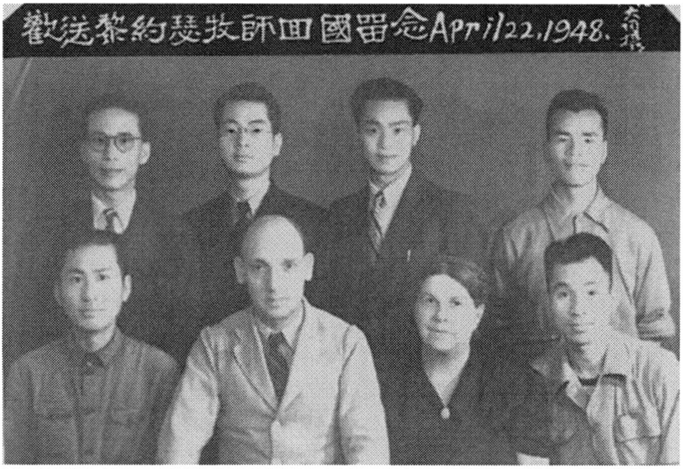

Joe had left Marian and the children safely in England and came back to join them some time before 1949 when all missionaries had to leave China.

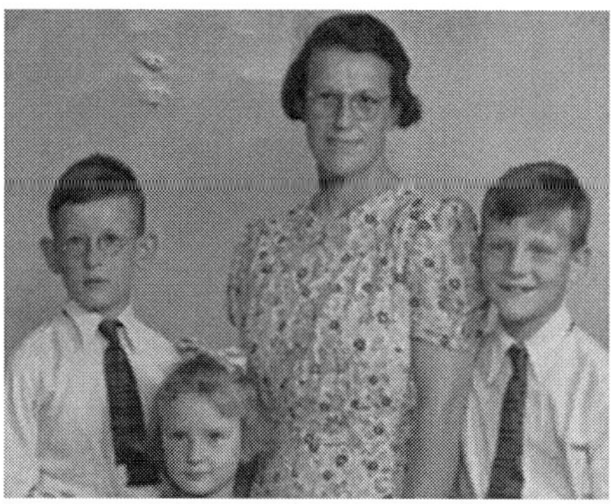

11
Dangerous times continued

'Little did they know what was to happen in Burma and China in the following years....'

In 1949 The People's Republic of China was established. Chairman Mao had a huge task ahead after years of conflict. As a child he had read stories of rebellions in China, and throughout the years of civil war and the Japanese invasion he had spent periods of time studying, writing and speaking at meetings, and adapting the ideas of Lenin and Karl Marx for China with its huge population of peasant farmers. The Party had come through years of struggle and had lost many members during the desperate days of *'The Long March'* in 1934.

Mao is praised for modernizing China, promoting the status of women, improving education and health care and housing. There were bans on foot binding and the smoking of opium. However there followed many developments and there are different interpretations of this period of history.

In the *'Let a Hundred Flowers Bloom'* campaign of 1956/7 artists and intellectuals were encouraged to criticize the Party. There are different views about the purpose of this movement, and there followed widespread suppression of counter-revolutionaries, particularly former members of the Kuomintang, businessmen, intellectuals and former employees of Western companies, many of whom were arrested and executed or sentenced to time in labour camps.

There were riots throughout the country. People were falsely accused and promises the CCP had made to former Kuomintang members that they would be forgiven for past associations were often ignored. Thousands attended rallies where public executions were carried out. In an article in Time Magazine in 1956 it was stated that in no previous war had so many people been destroyed in a short period, and that China was in a *'state of terror.'*

The land belonging to landlords and wealthy farmers was redistributed to poorer peasants. Some have admitted that at this time too many people were labelled as rich landlords and were at times deprived of land altogether and also that the executions of landowners were out of control. Opium crops were replaced with rice. Within the

Party there were different views about how change should be brought about, moderates thought it should be gradual and aiming towards industrialization, but Mao took control of agriculture, establishing collectives and forcing unpopular reforms which obliged farmers to attend political meetings and propaganda sessions often at a distance from their homes.

In 1956 there was widespread famine but people who spoke out against the agricultural policies were purged. The *Great Leap Forward* of 1958 planned the development of agriculture and industry, making use of cheap labour and avoiding the import of heavy machinery. Huge people's communes were established and run on authoritarian lines. Mao was convinced that China should follow its own path to communism and around this time the Soviet Union withdrew technical experts from China.

Steel production was increased but for a while it was based on what were known as *backyard steel furnaces* where peasants were only able to produce low quality pig iron out of scrap metal often which they had to procure themselves. Many workers were diverted for this work from other jobs and intellectuals lived in fear of voicing their views on this inefficient method. There were large scale water conservancy projects carried out without the guidance of trained engineers. Ill advised innovations were made in crop growing which generally led to decreased grain production. Local customs such as weddings funerals and religious rituals were outlawed and people were forced to attend political meetings. Homes were destroyed and people were weakened by hunger and exhaustion and many were humiliated, tortured and killed by party officials.

There were grain shortages at home but the export of grain continued. In 1959 the Yangtse River flooded large parts of eastern China and in 1960 there were droughts affecting some areas. In 1961 the export of grain was stopped and there were some imports from Canada and Australia. Estimates of how many millions of deaths resulted from this famine vary as do the assessments of its causes. The severity varied from region to region, but it was certainly one of the deadliest famines in the history of the world.

Despite personal risk some party members made the point that education and technical expertise were essential and that many of these experiments were a failure. In 1959 Mao stood down as Chairman of the PRC though he remained Chairman of the CPC. Power shifted to moderates led by Liu Shaoqi and Deng Xiaoping, who took effective control of the economy following 1959. For the time being many of the economic policies were reversed. Mao continued to contemplate Marxist-Leninist social theory, including the idea of *"continuous revolution".*

In 1966 Mao set in motion the *Cultural Revolution* the aims of which were to enforce communism by removing capitalist, traditional and cultural elements from Chinese society, and stop the development of a privileged class. The aim was to destroy 'the Four Olds' – old ideas, old culture, old customs and old habits. Many thousands of young people became Red Guards around the country and millions of people were persecuted, imprisoned, tortured, humiliated, made homeless and executed. Much that was connected with history was destroyed.

In the same year there was a radio report by the BBC which said that China was announcing plans for a *'new leap forward'* which was to follow a meeting of the Communist Party's Central Committee. The report said that Peking was determined to spread the words of leader Mao Tse-tung and purge those who followed capitalism. They quoted a news broadcast on Radio Peking which said the committee supported this programme which was described as *'the great proletarian cultural revolution'.* It later said that Chairman Mao had attempted to 'stimulate agricultural and industrial production' and that by organizing great communes he intended to release workers for production of steel. They reported that the plan did not work and grain output suffered, and there was production of shoddy, unwanted goods.

The BBC report quoted the expression - *"invigorating revolutionary atmosphere prevailing in the country"* and that according to Chinese News Agency reports '

'Chairman Mao received a tumultuous reception three days ago when he visited supporters in Peking and called on them to carry the great proletarian cultural revolution through to the end.'

It was also reported that 'thirty-five million copies of "The Selected Works of Mao Tse-tung" were to be printed within the next 18 months so his thoughts could be relayed to the masses said to be eagerly waiting to study and apply Mao's work. 'The Thoughts of Chairman Mao' or the 'Little Red Book' was published from about 1964 – 1976 and is one of the most printed books in history.

After his death in 1976 reformers gained power and the party's control over people's lives became less intrusive, with many communes disbanded and eventually China became a more mixed economy. Marian and Joe may have heard some of these radio broadcasts.

However it's unlikely there were any such reports from Burma. My parents were settled in England. They did their best to keep in touch with people they had known. Here is part of a letter in our mother's handwriting marked 'copy' on the back.

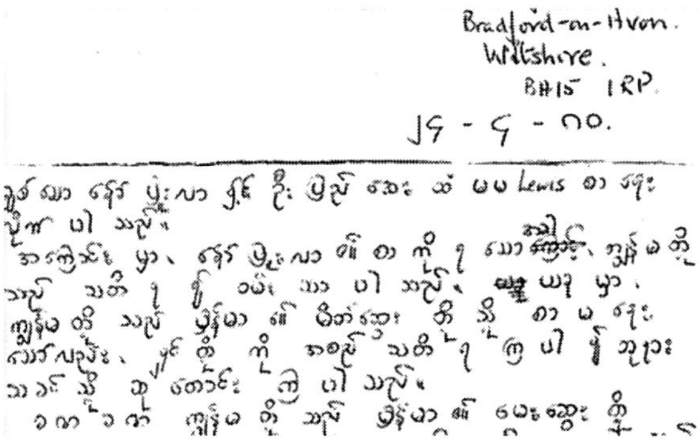

At this time there were ethnic struggles and also armed movements by various communist organisations. During the 1950's Burma recognized the People's Republic of China as a nation, but discriminated against the Chinese living in Burma and removed armed Kuomintang members, many of whom had fled over the border from Yunnan province. It accepted some foreign assistance in rebuilding the country after the war but soon came to reject foreign aid and sought to be impartial in world affairs.

Army Chief of Staff General Ne Win took over the government and his party won a large majority in the general elections in 1960. The Army saw communist organisations as a threat and continuing separatists movements were put down. It is thought there has been some persecution of Christians and destruction of churches. By 1966 all missionaries had to leave and Aunt Dorothy left around then.

In 1962 a peaceful student protest was violently suppressed. In 1963 many armed insurgents against the government were arrested and in March 1964 all opposition parties were banned. General Ne Win had a vision of a socialist state and established The Burma Socialist Programme Party (BSPP).His policies affected many entrepreneurs including the Chinese and many thousands left Burma at this time. This coincided with the period of chaos and fear in China under Chairman Mao.

This view of a street in Rangoon with the Sule pagoda is dated 1966,

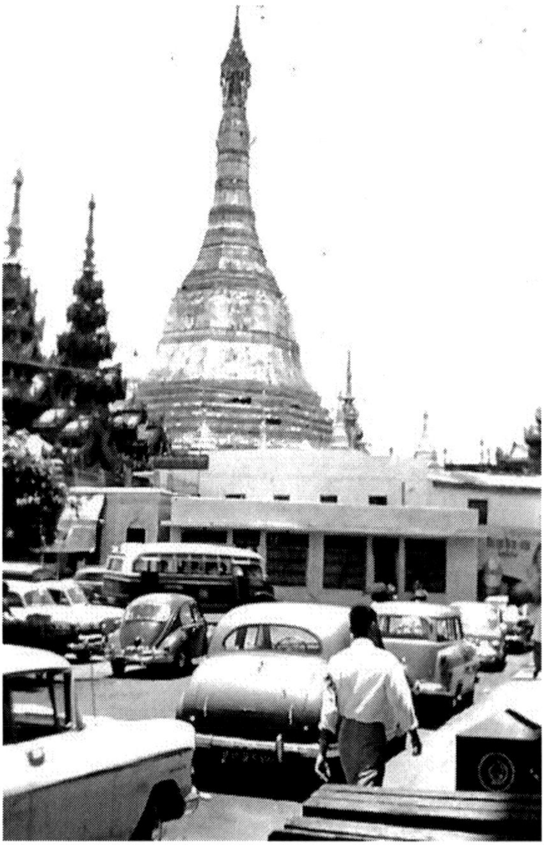

In 1974 anti government protests were suppressed at the funeral of U Thant who had been a close advisor to former Prime Minister U Nu in

the 1950s. People felt that he was denied the state funeral that he deserved as the former Secretary-General of the United Nations. Rice and mineral exports fell dramatically. Strikes against corruption, inflation and food shortages were suppressed.

A new constitution in 1974 resulted in the creation of a People's Assembly (Pyithu Hluttaw) and *The Socialist Republic of the Union of Burma* was adopted from 1974 to 1988. Despite its natural resources and fertile plains Burma became one of the world's poorest nations.

(photos 2012)

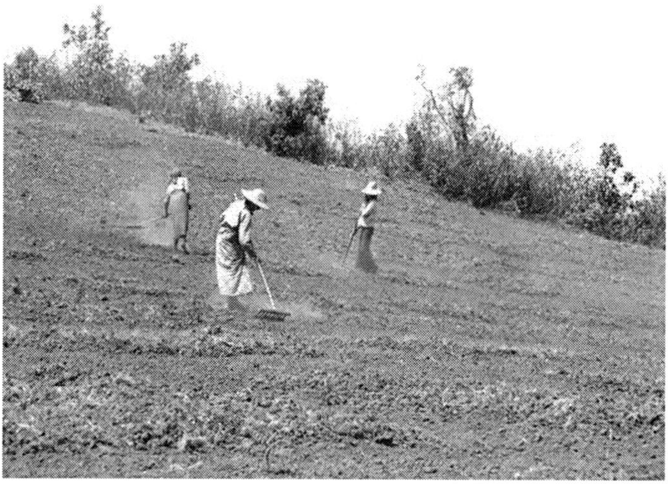

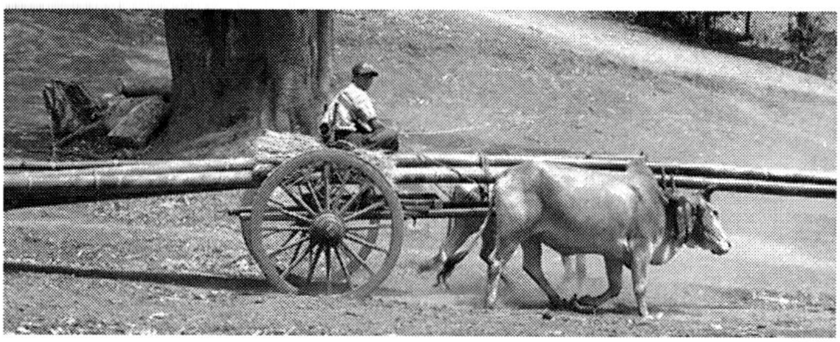

In March 1976 over 100 students were arrested for holding a peaceful ceremony to mark the centenary of the birth of Thawing Kodaw Hmaing, a great Burmese poet and writer who worked for peace and national reconciliation and is buried in a mausoleum at the foot of the Shwedagon Pagoda.

Inside a monastery in 2012

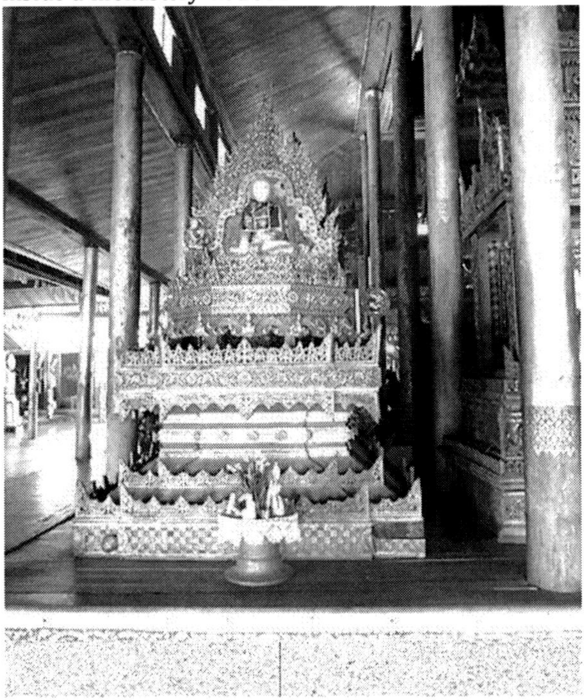

Many students and monks were thrown into prison for long periods of time. People lost their homes through government building projects and there was the use of forced labour, including children.

Aung San Suu Kyi returned to Burma from England in 1988 to care for her sick mother and this coincided with the stepping down of General Ne Win. Eight is a significant number in Burma, with the noble Eightfold parth of Buddhism and the eight victories of Lord Buddha. The 8888 uprising was started by students in Rangoon on August 8th

1988. Many thousands of monks, children, students and working people demonstrated against the regime and on 26 August Aung San Suu Kyi addressed thousands of people at a mass rally in front of the Shwedagon Pagoda calling for a democratic government. In September, there was a military coup by the SLORC (*State Law and Order Restoration Council*) led by General Saw Maung. Thousands of people died and were imprisoned. In 1989 SLORC declared martial law after widespread protests.

The military government finalised plans for People's Assembly elections on 31 May 1989 and in that year the official name of Burma became the *'Union of Myanmar'.* During this period however there was some encouragement of private sector growth and foreign investment, and some businesses were able to become re-established, including some run by Chinese Burmese.

In May 1990, the government held *free elections* for the first time in almost 30 years and despite the fact that the National League for Democracy (NLD) won 392 out of a total 489 seats the military refused to give up power, and Aung San Sui Kyi and the Chairman, U Tin U were placed under house arrest, and other members of the party, U Win Tin and U Kyi Maung were also arrested.

The gate to Aung San Suu Kyi's house, 2012

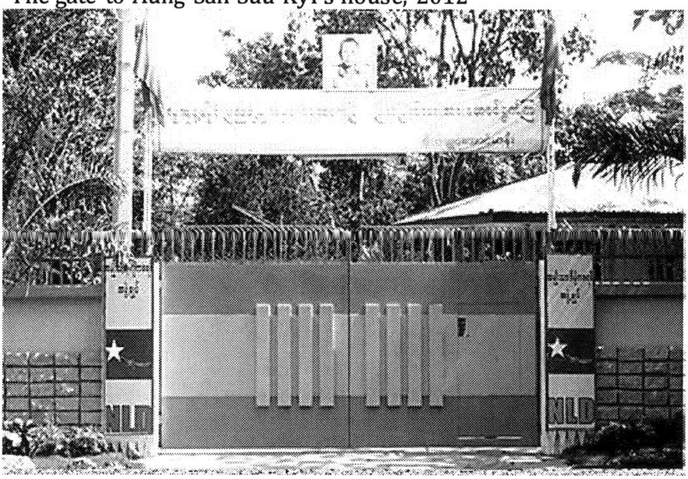

On 23 June 1997, Burma became a member of the Association of Southeast Asian Nations (ASEAN).The government continued to rule the nation as SLORC until 1997, and then as the *State Peace and Development Council* (SPDC). The military junta which had moved the national capital from Yangon to a site near Pyinmana officially named the newly built modern capital Naypyidaw, meaning *'city of the kings'* in March 2006.

In 2007 the SPDC had decided to remove fuel subsidies and the price of petrol and gas rose dramatically. While many people were starving the military authorities were enjoying great wealth. This and other injustices and difficulties lay behind demonstrations which grew into the largest anti-government protests for 20 years. They were led by monks and reports on television reached the world outside.

On September 22nd thousands of monks marched in Rangoon and Mandalay and other townships, and Aung San Suu Kyi made an appearance at her gate despite still being under house arrest. Later there were conflicting reports that she had been moved to Insein prison or other locations. Peaceful marches were suppressed by the authorities with many monks and protesters arrested and taken away. On September 24th the crowds of protesters grew to tens of thousands.

There was a very large demonstration at Kyaukpadaung, near Mandalay, with about 30,000 led by around 1,000 monks. This was peaceful despite the presence of the military. President George W. Bush introduced sanctions against the military government and the Dalai Lama gave his blessing to the monks. On September 25th army trucks were placed at the Shwedagon Pagoda and riot police were employed to disperse the crowds. On September 27th security forces started to raid monasteries across the country, arresting monks. The radio station Democratic voice of Burma reported that nine civilians, including the Japanese photographer Kenji Nagai had been shot and killed.

The government cut off Internet access and people caught carrying cameras were beaten up. There were continuing and conflicting reports about more demonstrations and the violent treatment of monks and civilians, with some residents in Myitkyina being forced to attend rallies designed to manufacture support for the government. For some days soldiers were positioned at many locations in Rangoon to stop further protests.

The U N Special Envoy Ibrahim Gambari arrived in Yangon and was due to fly immediately to Naypyidaw to talk with the junta generals. There were conflicting reports about his visit and it is thought he was allowed to meet with Aung San Suu Kyi after he returned from Naypyidaw. It is reported that Wen Jiabao, the Premier of the People's Republic of China announced:

"China hopes all parties concerned in Myanmar show restraint, resume stability through peaceful means as soon as possible, promote domestic reconciliation and achieve democracy and development".

The United Nations Human Rights Council met to discuss the situation in Myanmar and passed a resolution deploring the violent repression of peaceful demonstrations, and urging the release of all those arrested during the demonstrations.

Another report suggested that up to 10,000 people, many of them monks had been "rounded up for interrogation in recent days". Diplomats from the United States visited a number of monasteries and found them empty or guarded by solders. General Ye Min Tun felt he was forced to resign from the military regime. Amnesty International expressed grave concerns about the lives and the safety of those imprisoned.

There was a 'pro government' rally on October 13th which many were forced to attend. There were reports that some generals and hundreds of soldiers had been jailed for refusing to shoot and beat monks and civilians during protests. There were widely varying reports about the numbers imprisoned and killed. Tougher sanctions on Burma were proposed by various countries and companies, with many organisations expressing concern and demanding the release of prisoners, many of whom were given long sentences. President Bush made the statement:

"Monks have been beaten and killed. Thousands of pro-democracy protesters have been arrested. Burma's rulers continue to defy the world's just demand to stop their vicious persecution. We are confident that the day is coming when freedom's tide will reach the shores of Burma."

There were reports that many ethnic minorities were fleeing to India to get away from being forced to join pro-government rallies, and Christians were persecuted. The government continued to try and block the Internet but many people still managed to gain access and images of the protests reached mainstream news organisations.

photo 2012

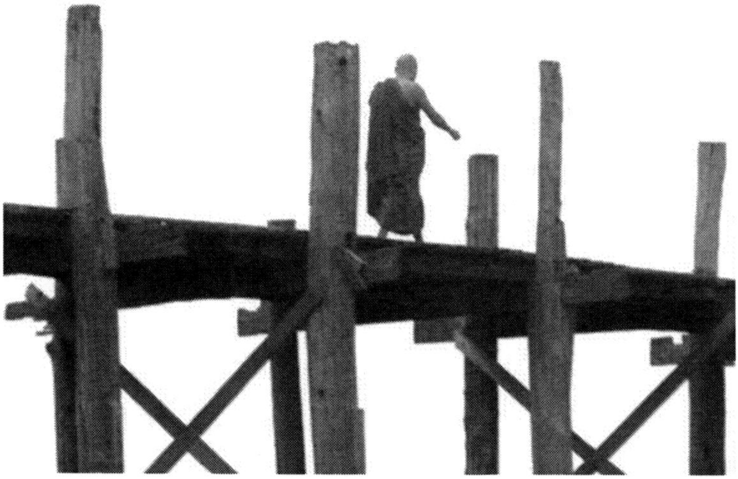

During these years the daily lives of ordinary people were affected by intrusive laws, such as the need to report the presence of guests in one's house to the Law and Order Restoration Council before 9 o'clock in the evening. Also people leaving their own homes also had to report to LORC where they were going.

The authorities had the right to check who was in any house at any time, resulting in harassment at any hour of the day or night, and failure to declare up to date information about guests could result in fines and the imprisonment of members of the family. People known to offer hospitality to NLD members were probably watched closely. Families of political activists lived in constant fear of the authorities arriving suddenly to interrogate them and interfere in their lives.

Children could grow up with the fear of losing one or both parents, and with limited rights to visit them in prison. Feeding one's family and guests was difficult because of severe inflation in Burma affecting the living standards of many people.

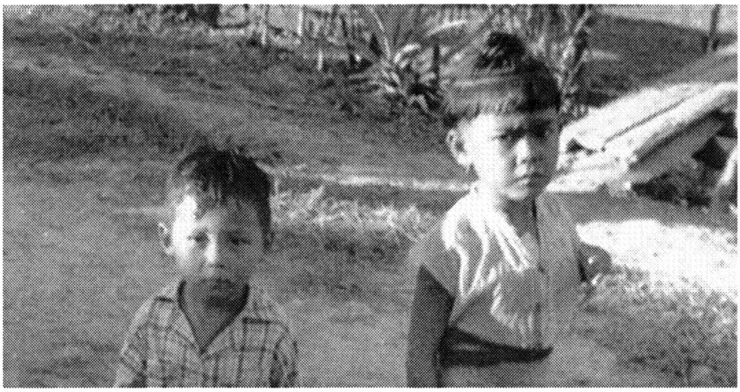

There was support for the NLD throughout the country. Traditional actors, singers and dancers often perform at Buddhist festivals and their songs can be satirical, and when this happened at a particular NLD celebration the authorities became uneasy – there is a report that the comedians U Pa Pa Lay and U Lu Zaw were taken away after one such performance.

In May 2008 there was the worst natural disaster in Burmese history when Cyclone Nargis caused extensive damage particularly in the densely populated Irrawaddy Delta, with an estimated 200,000 people dead or missing, and as many as one million left homeless. It is difficult to believe the reports that in the days after this disaster the government hindered aid in the form of food and medicine and other supplies from reaching the people.

A new constitution in 2008 reserved a quarter of seats in both parliamentary chambers for the military, and it stated that three ministerial posts must be held by serving generals. The country was renamed *The Republic of the Union of Myanmar*. In 2010 there was another *'General Election'* and observers described the day as peaceful though there were allegations of irregularities in polling stations. The military backed *Union Solidarity and Development Party* declared victory and this result was declared fraudulent by the United Nations.

Since 2011 there have been some reforms with a change in government under President Thein Sein. In December 2012 he travelled to Ratnagiri and paid homage at the run-down tomb of King Thibaw and met the late monarch's descendants. He is the first head of Burmese government to visit the grave.

IMAGES OF MYANMAR IN 2012

The Burmese tour guide

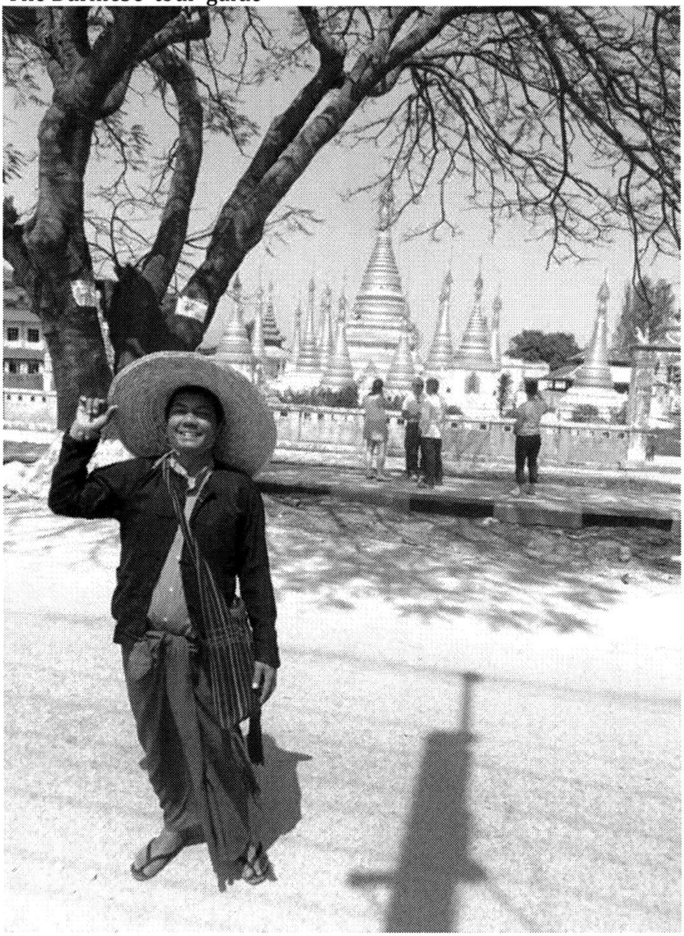

Old colonial buildings, Rangoon

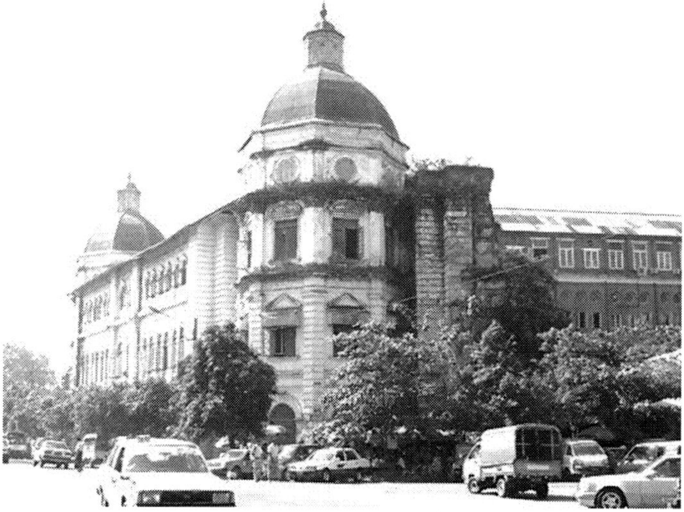

A recent view of the Sule pagoda

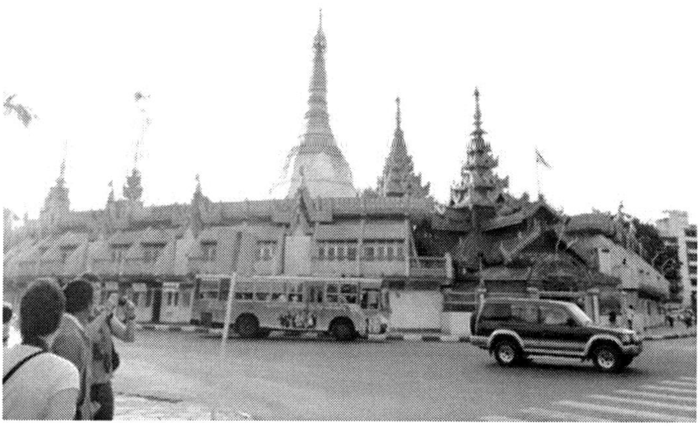

Inside a pagoda

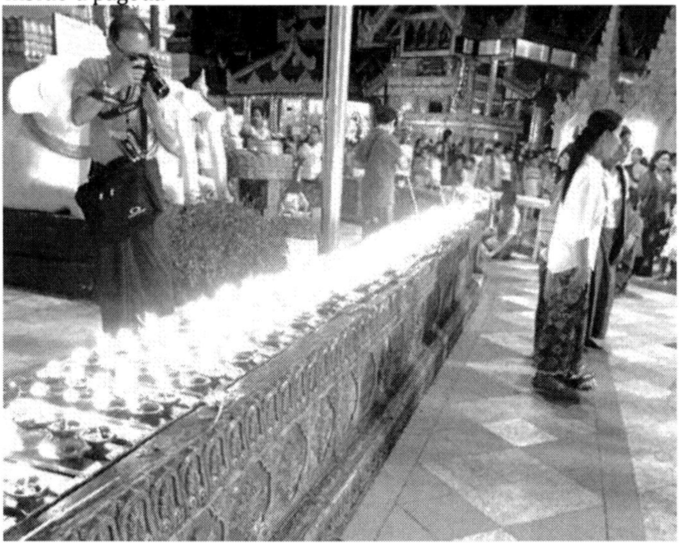

The railway station

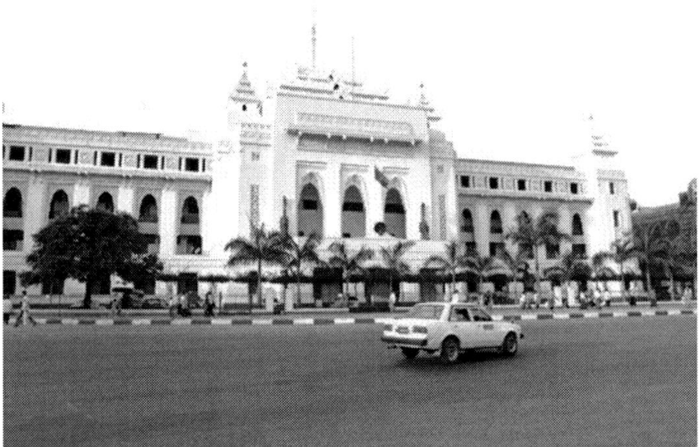

Boat on the lake

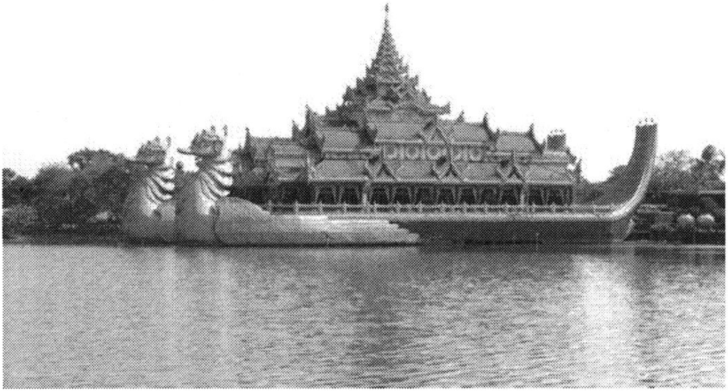

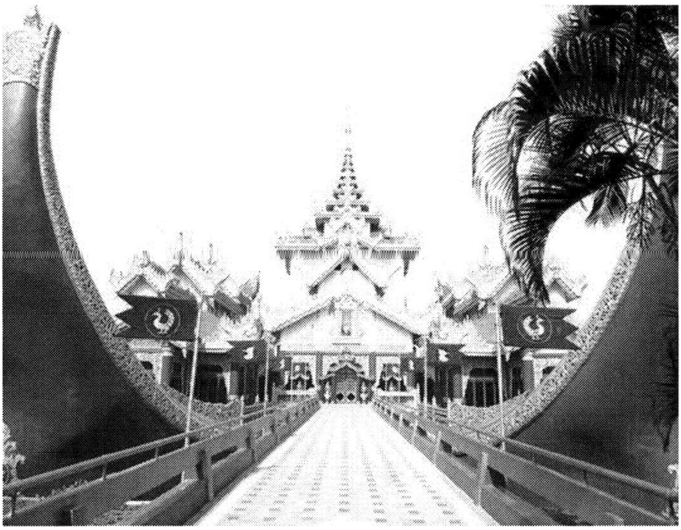

Traditional music

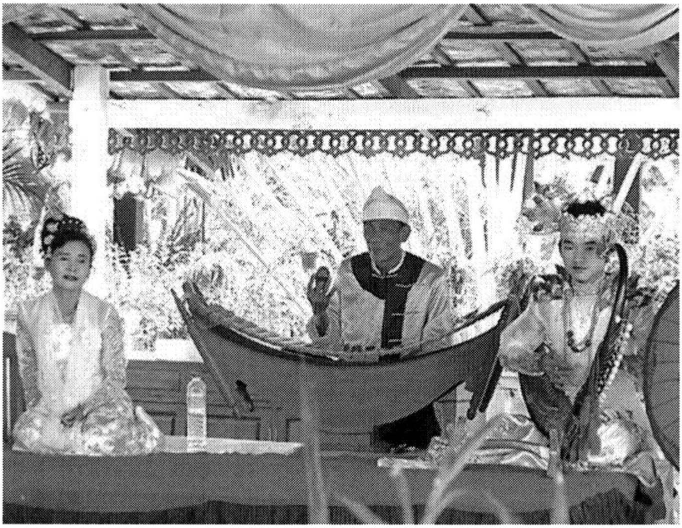

Main highway to Naypidaw the new capital city

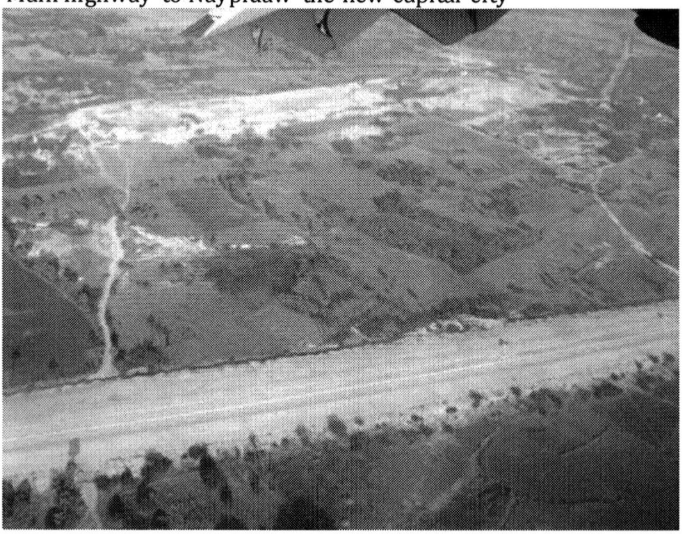

Working on the roads in country areas, seen from a bus

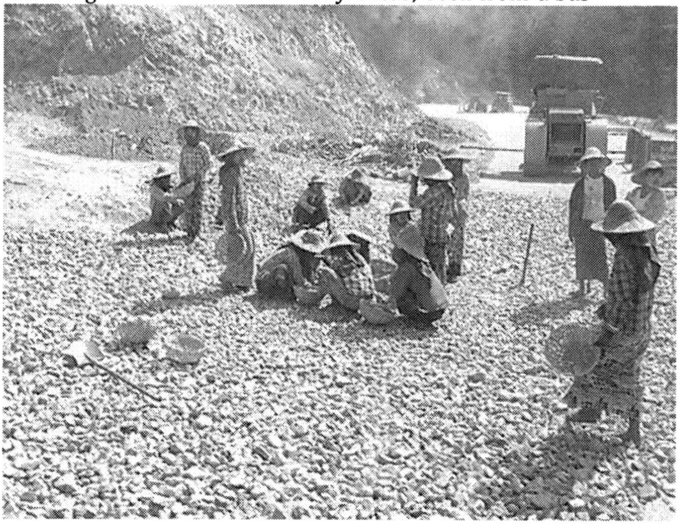

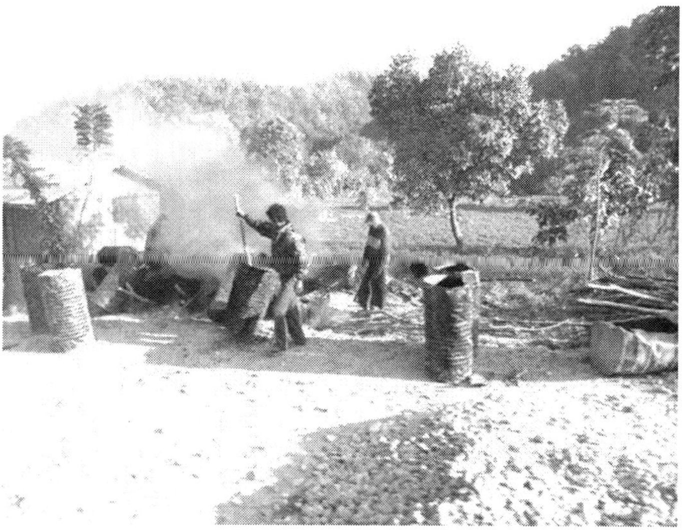

Bagan - views of many ancient temples

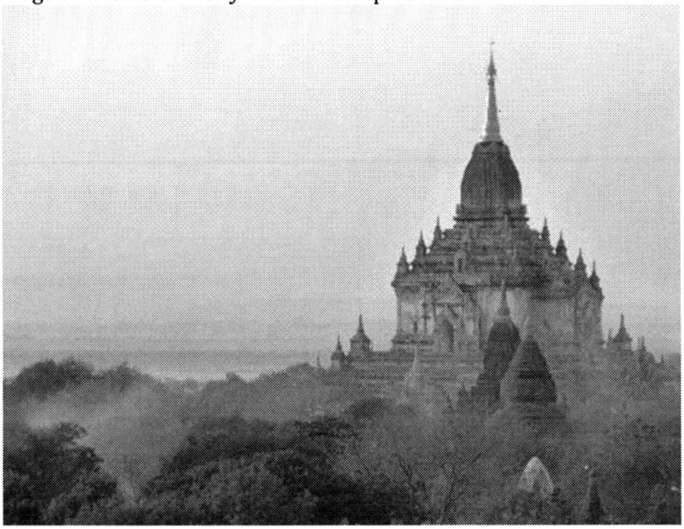

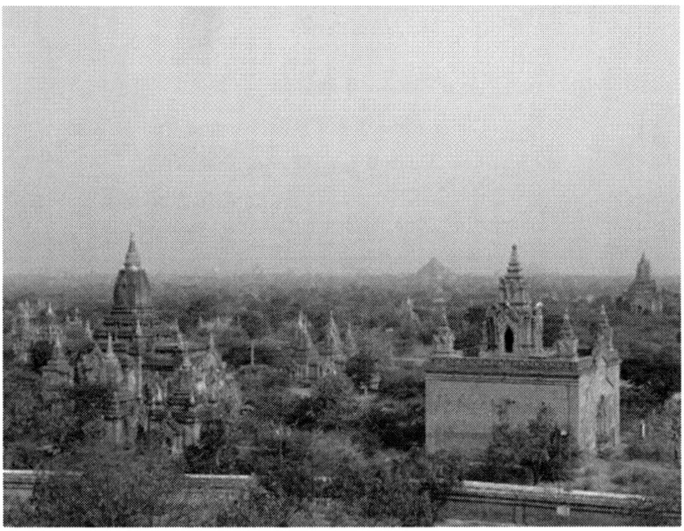

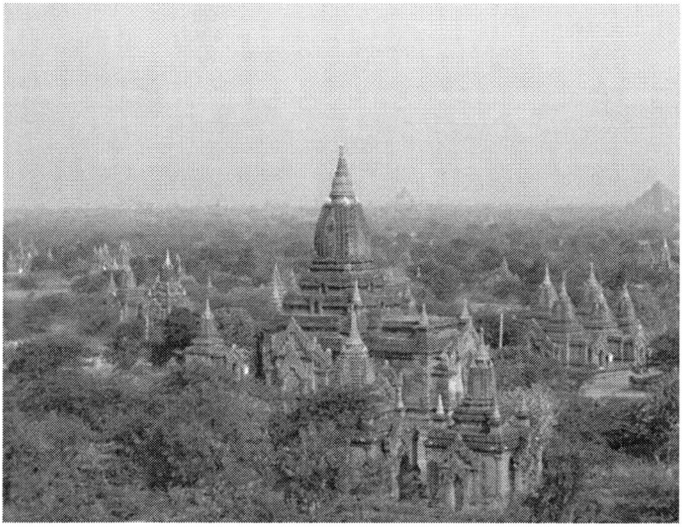

Views at a hotel

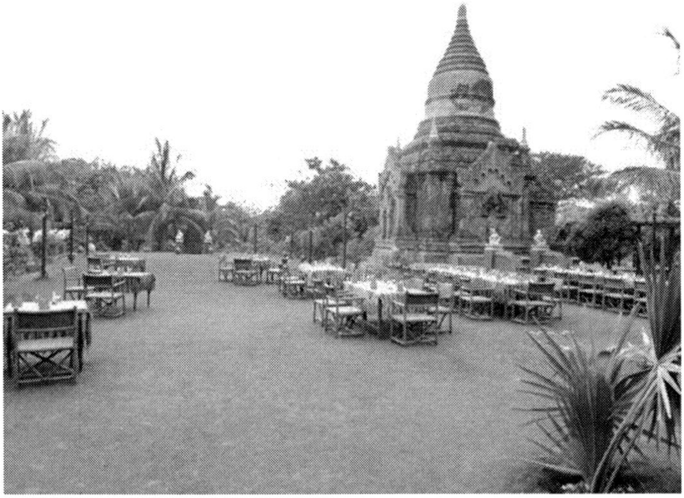

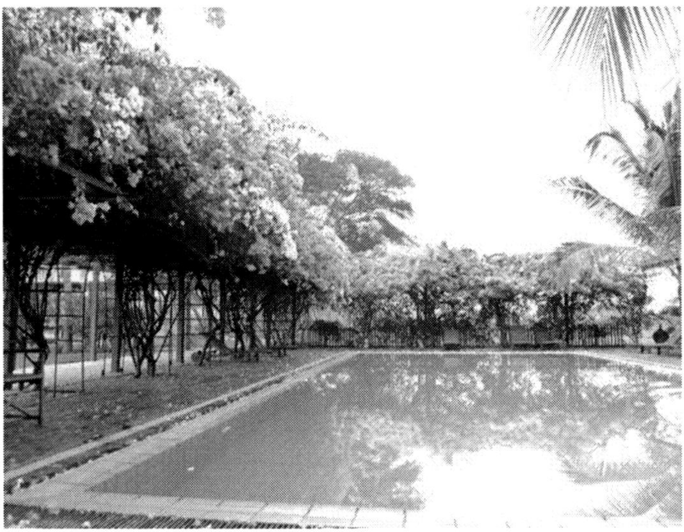

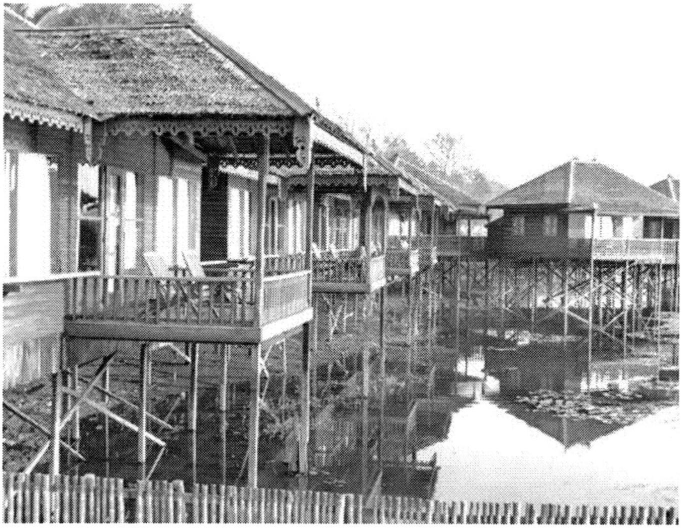

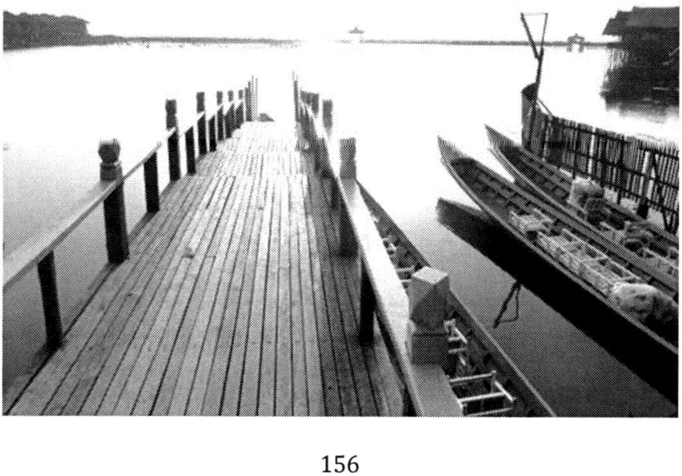

Restaurant on Inle Lake

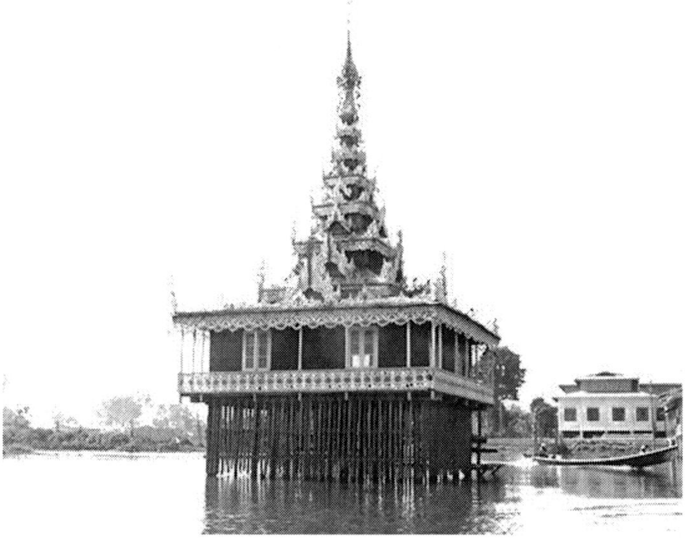

Views of Inle Lake

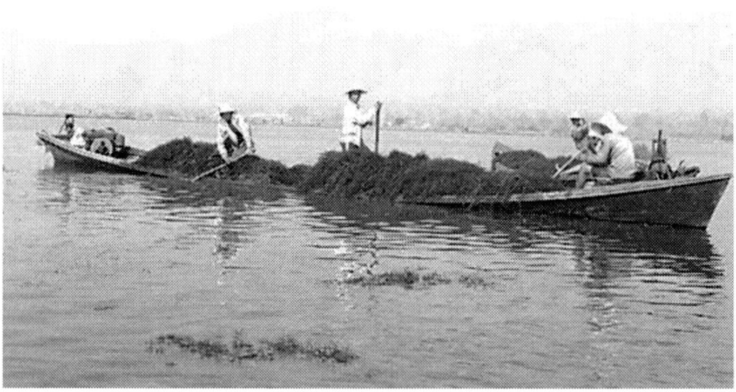

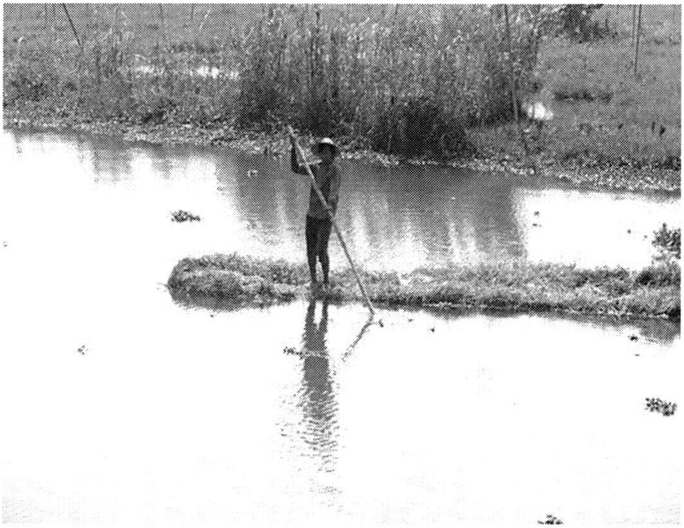

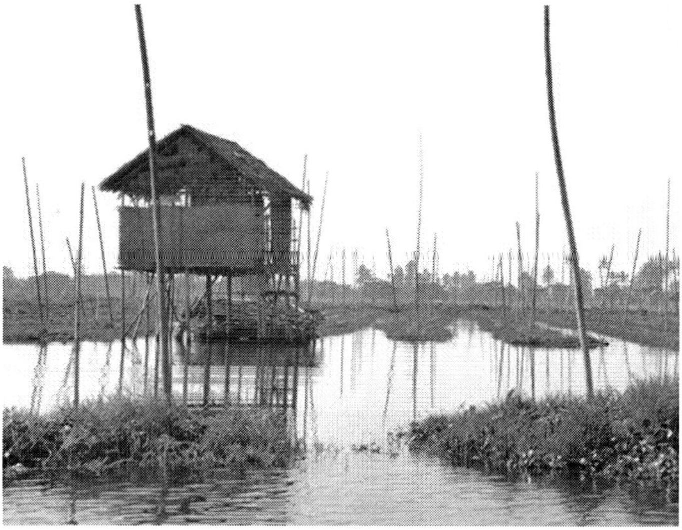

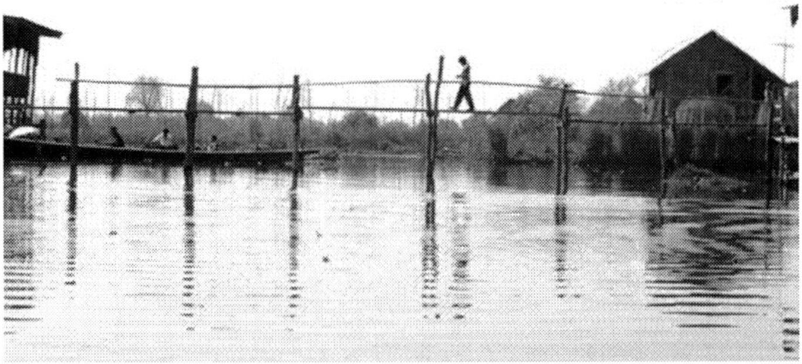

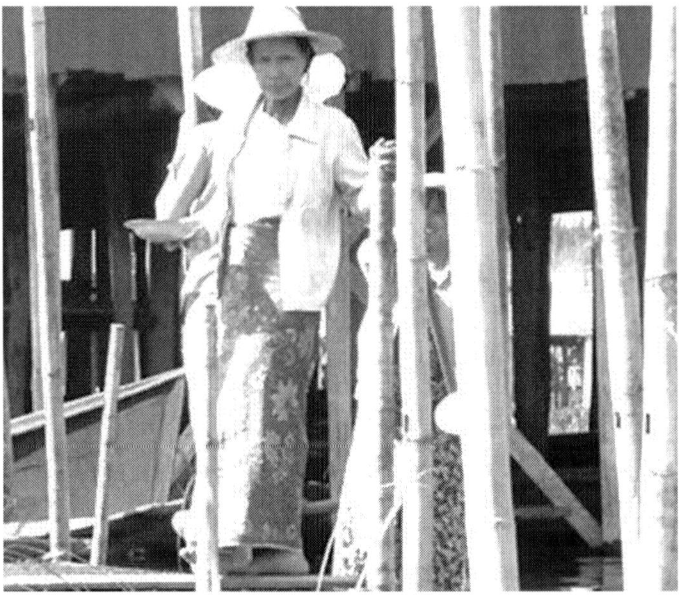

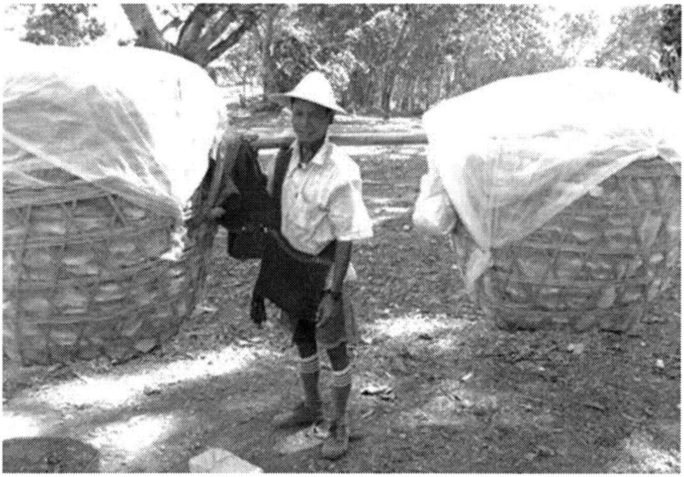

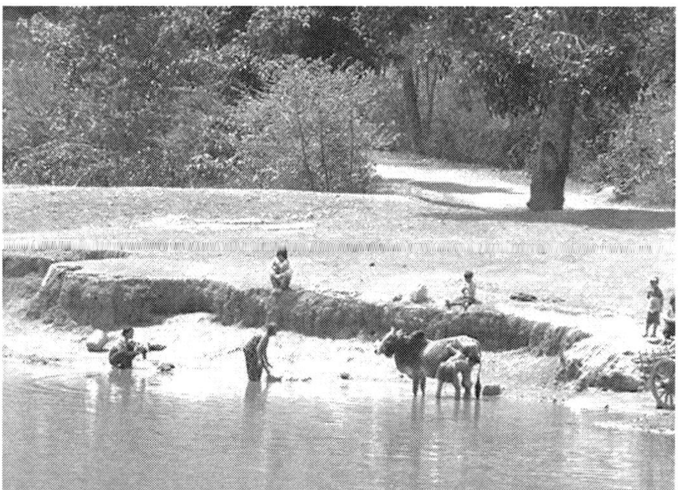

A teak monastery

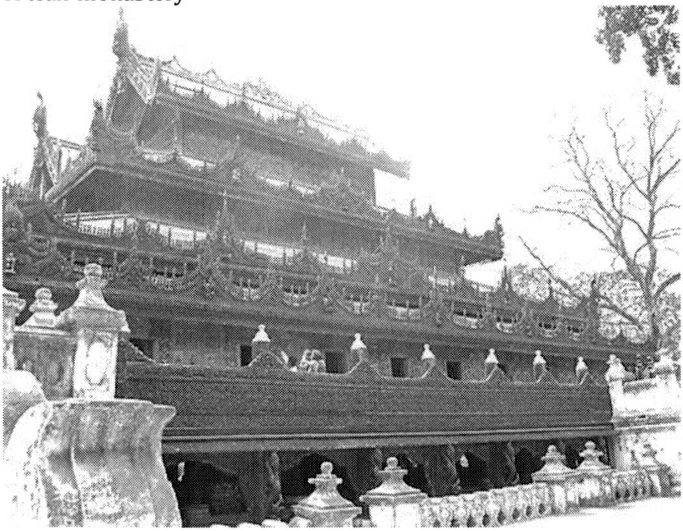

Many small pagodas

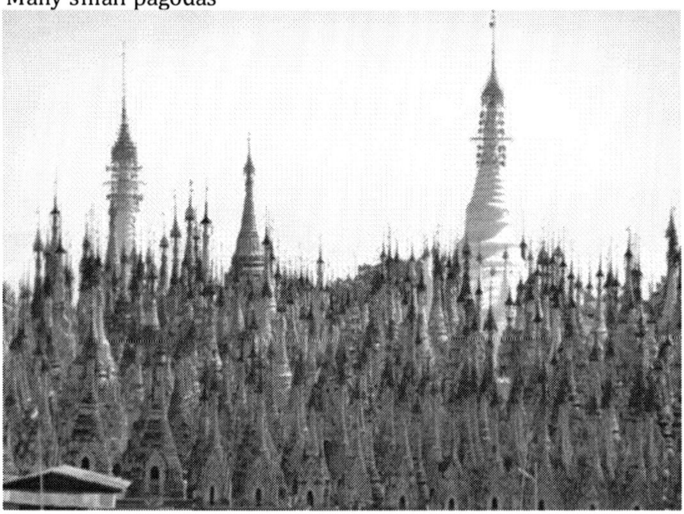

There is a collection of over 700 stone slabs inscribed with Buddhist teaching

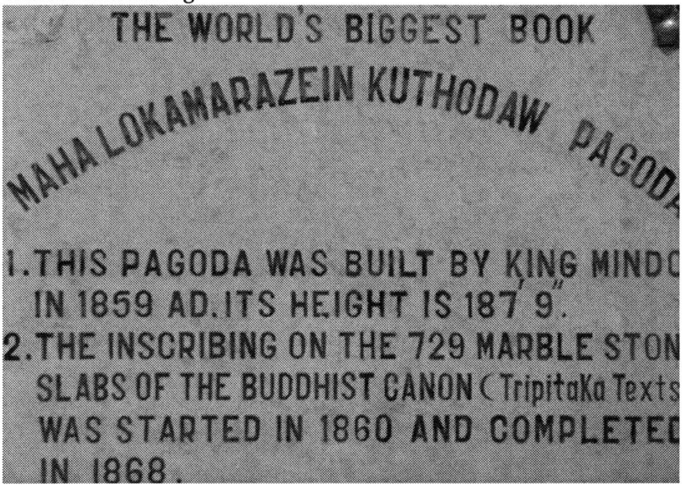

The giant Mingun bell

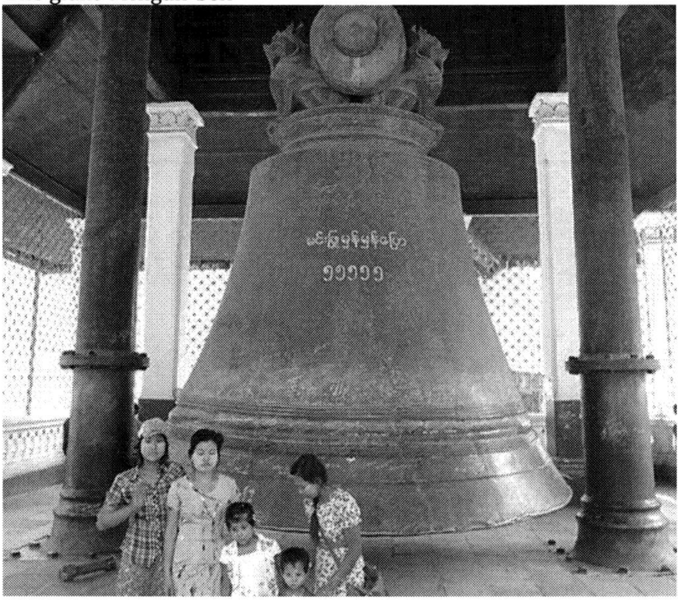

Inside a cave at Pindaya with Buddhist statues from the 18th and 19th centuries

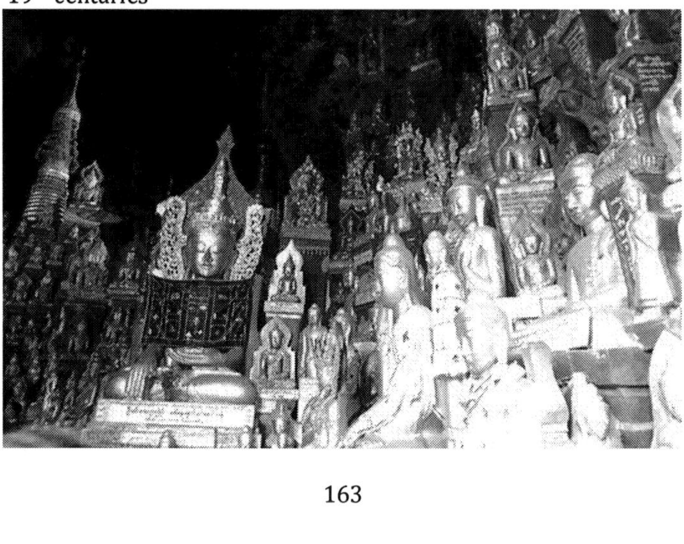

King Mindon was the father of the last king of Burma, King Thibaw

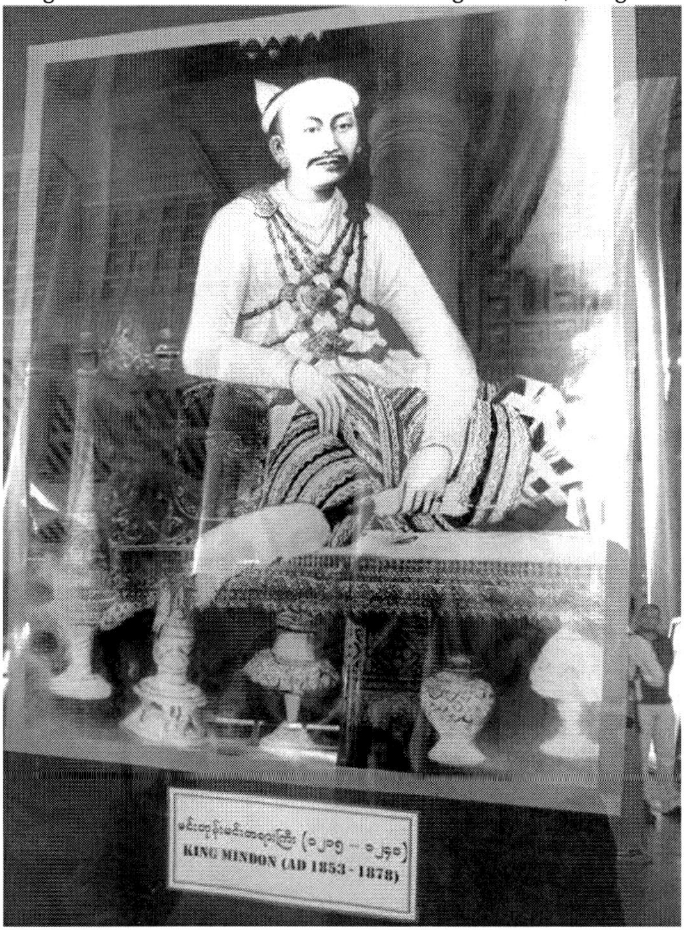

Gold is used extensively throughout Burma to beautify pagodas

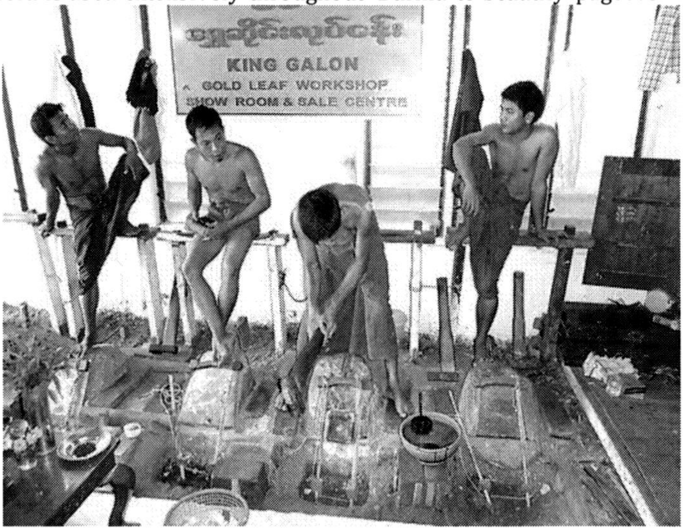

Monks setting off in the early morning as they have done for centuries

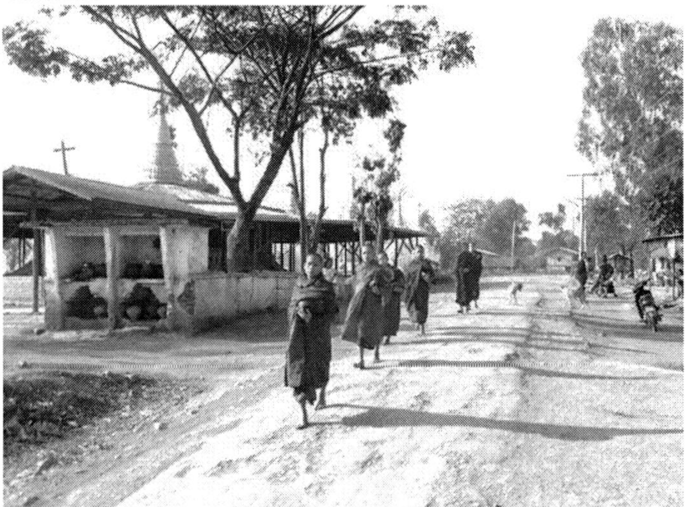

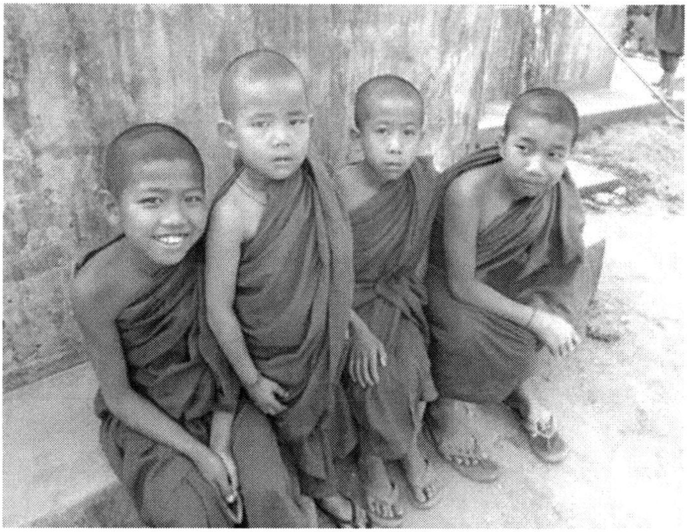

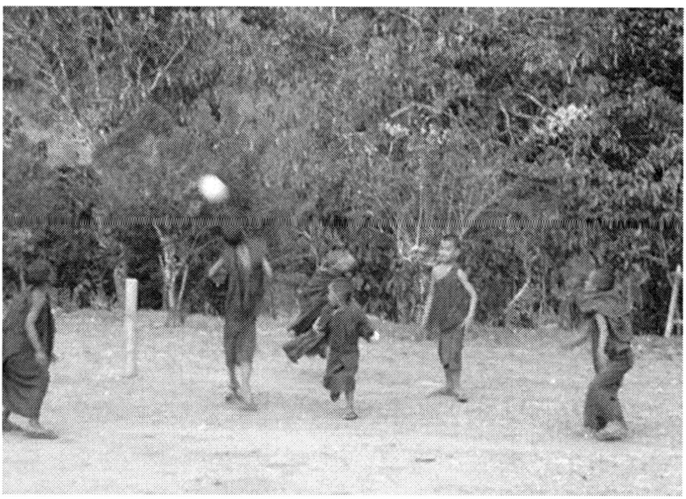

The 200 year old teak bridge at Amarapura near Mandalay is over two kilometres long

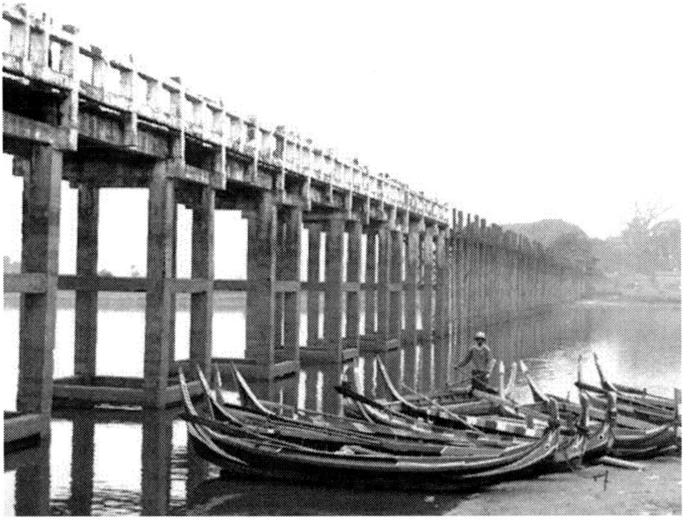

View from the Irrawaddy

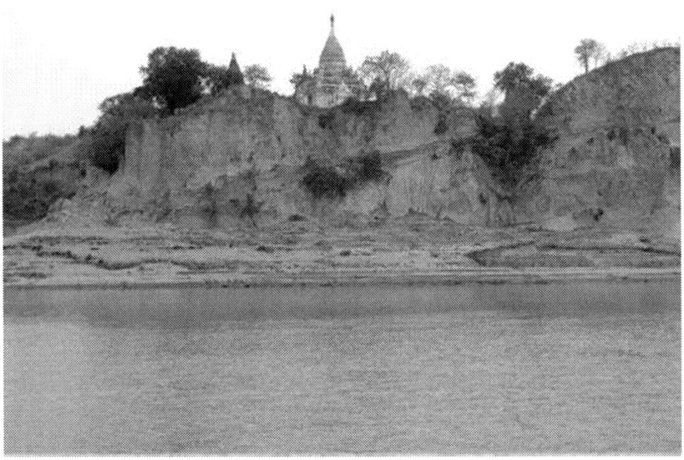

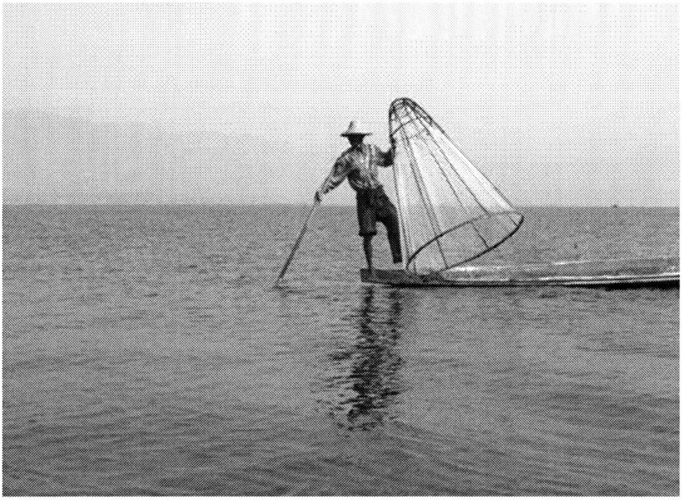

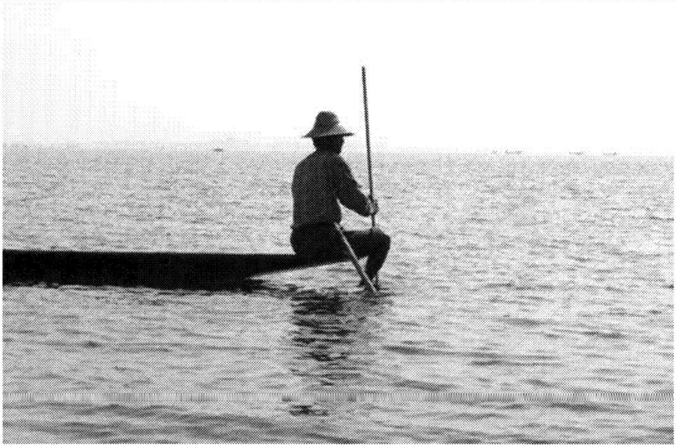

'Memory is a net; one finds it full of fish when one takes it from the brook; but a dozen miles of water have run through it without sticking.'

'Nothing is the beginning,
there was always more that had happened before'

Also by this author

A short book - *Historic photographs from Burma 1937 – 1966*

which contains further images from Aunt Dorothy's collection

ISBN 978 0 9926694 1 6